# Table of Contents

1. Introduction to Transformers ................................................................................................4

   1.1. Preliminaries .....................................................................................................................4

      1.1.1. Softmax Activation Function ....................................................................................4

      1.1.2. Information Retrieval ..................................................................................................5

      1.1.3. Dot-Product Similarity ...............................................................................................6

      1.1.4. Encoder-Decoder Paradigm .....................................................................................6

   1.2. The Transformer Architecture ...........................................................................................7

      1.2.1. Encoder Stack ...........................................................................................................8

         1.2.1.1. Pre-processing ..................................................................................................9

            1.2.1.1.1. Tokenization ..............................................................................................9

            1.2.1.1.2. Word Embeddings ...................................................................................10

            1.2.1.1.3. Positional Encoding ...............................................................................11

         1.2.1.2. Encoder Architecture........................................................................................12

            1.2.1.2.1. Self-Attention Mechanism .....................................................................12

            1.2.1.2.2. Multi-head Attention ..............................................................................16

            1.2.1.2.3. Residual Connections and Layer Normalization .....................................19

            1.2.1.2.4. Feed-forward Network (FFN) ..................................................................20

         1.2.1.3. Encoder Stack Operation .................................................................................22

      1.2.2. Decoder Stack .........................................................................................................22

         1.2.2.1. Pre-processing .................................................................................................24

         1.2.2.2. Decoder Architecture .......................................................................................24

            1.2.2.2.1. Masked Self-attention .............................................................................24

            1.2.2.2.2. Cross-attention.......................................................................................26

            1.2.2.2.3. From Embeddings to Tokens ..................................................................27

         1.2.2.3. Decoder Stack Operation .................................................................................29

2. Language Modeling using Transformers .............................................................................31

   2.1. Preliminaries ...................................................................................................................31

      2.1.1. Language Models .....................................................................................................31

      2.1.2. GELU and Hyperbolic Tangent.................................................................................32

   2.2. BERT ...............................................................................................................................33

      2.2.1. Model.........................................................................................................................33

      2.2.2. WordPiece Tokenization............................................................................................34

      2.2.3. Pre-training ...............................................................................................................35

2.2.3.1. Masked Language Modeling..................................................................36

2.2.3.2. Next Sentence Prediction ....................................................................37

2.2.4. Fine-tuning ............................................................................................38

2.3. GPT ...............................................................................................................39

2.3.1. Model .....................................................................................................40

2.3.2. Byte-pair Encoding Tokenization..............................................................40

2.3.3. Unsupervised Pre-training........................................................................41

2.3.4. Supervised Fine-tuning ...........................................................................42

2.4. GPT-2 ............................................................................................................44

2.5. GPT-3 ............................................................................................................45

2.5.1. Model .....................................................................................................46

2.5.2. Pre-training.............................................................................................47

2.5.3. Performance............................................................................................47

2.6. GPT-3.5 and ChatGPT ....................................................................................49

3. The Vision Transformer .......................................................................................51

3.1. Preliminaries..................................................................................................52

3.1.1. Pre-Normalization and Post-Normalization ...............................................52

3.1.2. Multi-Layer Perceptron (MLP) and Classification Head..............................53

3.1.3. Network Fine-tuning ................................................................................53

3.1.4. Visual Task Adaptation Benchmark (VTAB).................................................54

3.2. Vision Transformer Architecture .....................................................................55

3.2.1. From Image to Embeddings .....................................................................56

3.2.1.1. Patch Tokens and Embeddings .............................................................56

3.2.1.2. Class Embedding...................................................................................58

3.2.1.3. Position Encoding .................................................................................58

3.2.2. Encoder Structure and Operations............................................................59

3.2.3. Standard Configurations...........................................................................60

3.2.4. Fine-tuning and Performance....................................................................61

3.2.5. Computational Complexity .......................................................................63

4. Shifted Window Transformers................................................................................65

4.1. The Swin Architecture ....................................................................................65

4.1.1. Token Generation ....................................................................................66

4.1.2. Swin Transformer Block ...........................................................................67

4.1.2.1. Windowed Multi-head Self-attention .....................................................67

4.1.2.2. Shifted-window Multi-head Self-attention ................................................ 69

4.1.2.3. Batched Window Processing ................................................................ 71

4.1.3. Relative Position Bias .......................................................................... 72

4.1.4. Hierarchical Feature Maps .................................................................... 74

4.1.5. Standard Configurations ...................................................................... 76

4.2. Swin Transformer Version 2 ........................................................................ 77

4.2.1. Model Capacity .................................................................................... 78

4.2.1.1. Post-normalization ............................................................................ 78

4.2.1.2. Scaled Cosine Attention .................................................................... 79

4.2.2. Window Resolution .............................................................................. 80

4.2.2.1. Log-spaced Coordinates .................................................................... 80

4.2.2.2. Continuous Relative Position Bias ...................................................... 81

4.2.3. Standard Configurations ...................................................................... 82

4.3. Training Vision Transformers – SimMIM ...................................................... 83

5. Swin Transformers in Action ......................................................................... 87

5.1. Image Classification .................................................................................... 87

5.2. Object Detection and Segmentation ............................................................ 88

5.2.1. Feature Pyramid Network ...................................................................... 88

5.2.2. Object Detection and Instance Segmentation ......................................... 90

5.2.3. Semantic Segmentation ........................................................................ 93

5.3. Image Restoration ...................................................................................... 95

5.3.1. SwinIR Architecture .............................................................................. 96

5.3.1.1. Local Feature Extraction .................................................................... 96

5.3.1.2. Deep Feature Extraction – Residual Swin Transformer Blocks ............. 97

5.3.2. Restoration Tasks ................................................................................ 98

5.3.2.1. Image Super-resolution ...................................................................... 98

5.3.2.2. Image Denoising ................................................................................ 100

5.3.2.3. JPEG Compression Artifact Removal .................................................. 100

References ........................................................................................................ 102

# 1. Introduction to Transformers

The Transformer architecture was introduced by Vaswani et al. [1] as a fresh approach to processing sequential data in Natural Language Processing (NLP) tasks. It is a novel architecture that aims to improve the performance of sequence-to-sequence tasks by providing a mechanism to efficiently extract long-range dependencies. The Transformer architecture was originally targeted for language processing applications such as machine language translation since they deal primarily with sequences of words. It has found widespread acceptance in this field due to its superior performance over previous architectures such as recursive neural networks (RNNs). The Transformer architecture has since been adapted to tasks in image processing, computer vision and audio processing, where it has shown promising results.

This chapter introduces the fundamental blocks of the original Transformer architecture and uses a specific language task to illustrate their operations. In certain instances, it also aims to present the intuition behind the structure of a block. Section 1.1 introduces prerequisites that are essential to the understanding of the Transformer architecture that is introduced in section 1.2. Section 1.2.1 describes the encoder half of the Transformer and section 1.2.2 explores the Transformer decoder. The end-to-end operation of the Transformer architecture is illustrated using a simple example of machine translation.

## 1.1. Preliminaries

This section introduces a few fundamental concepts that are essential to the understanding the rest of the Transformer architecture - the softmax activation function which is used extensively throughout the Transformer architecture, the concepts of query, key and value which are central ideas in the all-important self-attention mechanism, the use of the vector dot-product as a similarity metric and the basic encoder-decoder neural network architecture that is used to process sequential data.

### 1.1.1. Softmax Activation Function

The softmax activation function is used extensively in neural network architectures to generate a set of numbers that can be viewed as probabilities. The function operates on a vector of $N$ real numbers and generates a probability distribution over $N$ outcomes.

Denoting the real-valued vector input to the softmax function as $\vec{P} = [p_0, p_1, \ldots, p_{N-1}]$, the output of the function is expressed as follows:

$$Softmax(\vec{P}) = \left[\frac{e^{p_0}}{\sum_{j=0}^{N-1} e^{p_j}}, \frac{e^{p_1}}{\sum_{j=0}^{N-1} e^{p_j}}, \ldots, \frac{e^{p_{N-1}}}{\sum_{j=0}^{N-1} e^{p_j}}\right] = \vec{s}$$

It is often used as the last activation function of a neural network when there is a need to convert the output of the network to a distribution over a fixed set of known output classes (i.e. a network used for classification). This is because the components of the output vector satisfy the two necessary conditions for a valid probability distribution: $0 \leq s_i < 1$ for $0 \leq i \leq N - 1$, and $\sum_{i=0}^{N-1} s_i = 1$. The probability of $i^{\text{th}}$ target class is given by the entry $s_i$.

In a classification problem, the class with the highest calculated probability is usually chosen as the final output at inference time. The advantage of using the softmax function to generate the class probabilities is that it is a smooth function and is hence differentiable. This is a great asset since gradients can be easily calculated during the training of the neural network. In a general application, the outputs from the softmax function can also be used as a set of scaling factors to generate a weighted average of a group of observations. The softmax function is used for both of these purposes in the Transformer architecture.

## 1.1.2. Information Retrieval

The concept of *attention*, which is at the core of the Transformer architecture, borrows the terms *query*, *key* and *value* from the field of information retrieval. Therefore, it is informative to gain an understanding of these terms in their original contexts. Consider a database of records and a search application that looks up the best match for an input candidate record. Each record that is stored in the database has a data key associated with it. This key acts as a record identifier and could be made up of pieces of information that uniquely identify the record. When a candidate record is received by the application, a query is constructed based on the unique characteristics of that input record. The search operation then compares the query with each available key in the database using some sort of similarity metric. It then picks the key that is the "most similar" to the query and retrieves the corresponding record (or the value).

The attention mechanism uses the concepts of query, key and value to capture the dependencies between the words in the input sequence. The query, key and value vectors are created for every input word and the vector dot-product is used as the similarity metric between each pair of query and key vectors. The attention mechanism is described in detail in section 1.2.1.

### 1.1.3. Dot-Product Similarity

Consider two vectors $\vec{a} = [a_0, a_1, ..., a_{M-1}]$ and $\vec{b} = [b_0, b_1, ..., b_{M-1}]$ in $M$-dimensional space (i.e., $\vec{a}, \vec{b} \in \mathbb{R}^{1 \times M}$, where $\mathbb{R}$ is the set of all real numbers). The dot-product (or inner-product) between the two vectors is computed as $\vec{a}.\vec{b} = \sum_{i=0}^{M-1} a_i b_i$. Alternatively, the geometric definition of the vector dot-product is given by $\vec{a}.\vec{b} = \|\vec{a}\|\|\vec{b}\| \cos\theta$, where $\|\vec{a}\| = \sqrt{\sum_{i=0}^{M-1} a_i^2}$ and $\|\vec{b}\| = \sqrt{\sum_{i=0}^{M-1} b_i^2}$ are the lengths (Euclidean norms) of the vectors and $\theta$ is the angle between the vectors in the *plane formed by the two vectors and the origin* of the $M$-dimensional vector space. The terminology used in this document is that vector $\vec{a}$ has a size of $1 \times M$ and a length of $\|\vec{a}\|$.

If the two vectors $\vec{a}$ and $\vec{b}$ have identical Euclidean norms of 1.0, their dot product is equal to the cosine of the angle between them and has a maximum value of 1.0 when the vectors are aligned (i.e., they are the same vector). The dot-product decreases as the angle between the vectors increases and has a value of zero for $\theta = \frac{\pi}{2}$, in which case the two vectors are orthogonal to each other. The dot-product can therefore be used as a measure of the alignment between any two vectors $\vec{a}$ and $\vec{b}$. The concept can be similarly extended to vectors that have non-unity norms (magnitudes not equal to 1.0) in which case the dot-product additionally captures the relationship between the lengths of the two vectors.

In the context of the Transformer architecture, dot-products are computed between query and key vectors that are generated by projecting the inputs words onto a 512-dimensional space. The vectors in this case are assured to have unequal lengths and non-unity norms, and the dot-products that are computed for pairs of these vectors are normalized using the softmax function. Each normalized result is used as a measure of correlation or dependency between the respective pairs of vectors.

### 1.1.4. Encoder-Decoder Paradigm

Sequences are encountered frequently in NLP tasks such as neural machine translation, text prediction, text analysis and sentiment analysis. They may involve sentences in one language that need to be translated to another language or could be a paragraph of words (for example, in a product review) whose sentiment needs to be classified. Traditional multi-layer neural networks are geared towards processing data groups that are independent of each other, and therefore lack the ability to capture explicit correlations between different portions of the sequence through time. This has led to the development of newer network architectures such as recursive neural networks (RNN), long-short term memory (LSTM) and gated recurrent units (GRU) for sequence processing and language modeling.

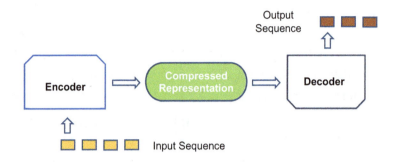

**Figure 1.1** Encoder-decoder Architecture used in Sequence Processing.

These architectures consist of two parts, an encoder and a decoder, as shown in figure 1.1. The encoder consumes the input data *sequentially* (one word at a time), accumulates contextual information and generates a final compressed representation. Depending on the application, the decoder could either wait for the entire input sequence to be encoded before it starts producing an output (e.g., text sentiment analysis) or could begin operating with a short lag (e.g., language translation). The size of the output sequence could be the same as or different from the size of the input sequence.

The key to the success of such an architecture is the ability of the encoder to efficiently capture both long-term and short-term dependencies between the words in the input sequence. The RNN, LSTM and GRU architectures have, in that order, improved upon this key aspect of the encoder. However, it has been proven that the NLP performances of even the best versions of these networks start to fall off at moderate lengths of the input sequence. In comparison, the Transformer architecture encodes the entire input sequence at once and this compressed representation is available to the decoder at every decoding step. Thus, it is able to better capture long-term dependencies and yield superior performance even with long input sequences.

## 1.2. The Transformer Architecture

The original Transformer model proposed in [1] is shown in figure 1.2. It is an encoder-decoder architecture that was introduced as a means to capture long-range dependencies in large sequences. As discussed in the sections below, the Transformer architecture is able to produce superior performance by encoding the entire input sequence at once, rather than in discrete time steps, and by utilizing the novel self-attention mechanism to successfully capture long-range dependencies between words. As a result, Transformers have gained a lot of attention in the NLP world and have since also been used to address problems in the field of Computer Vision.

The following sections discuss in detail the originally proposed architecture for the Transformer model. Since Transformers were designed for applications in the field of NLP, the architecture is most effectively described by using an example in that field. The rest of this document uses a

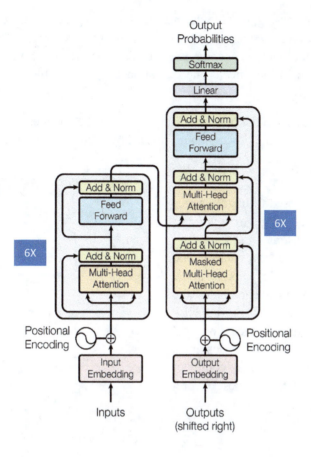

**Figure 1.2** The Original Transformer Architecture (modified from [1]).

running example of neural machine translation to illustrate the working of the Transformer. The example task is the translation of a simple sentence in English – My favorite animal is the cat - to French using a Transformer model that has been trained to perform this task. Note that the input sequence in such a task is typically a paragraph and not a single sentence, but this simple example is sufficient for the purpose of this discussion.

## 1.2.1. Encoder Stack

The encoder half of the Transformer is actually a serial stack of six identical encoder blocks (or layers). Except for the first encoder in the stack, every encoder operates on the outputs of the previous encoder. The input sequence is pre-processed to generate continuous-valued vectors that are fed to the first encoder. This encoder produces continuous-valued vectors which are consumed by the second encoder to produce another set of continuous-valued vectors, and so on. This process continues until the last encoder in the stack has generated a set of output vectors. These vectors undergo further post-processing, outside the encoder stack, to generate representations for use by the decoder. The processed encoder outputs correspond to the compressed representation in the earlier discussion on the generic encoder-decoder architecture. Note that in the Transformer architecture, the entire input sequence is encoded at once as a single block of data to generate this compressed representation.

The following sections discuss the pre-processing stages of the encoder, the sub-layers within an individual encoder layer and the processing performed by each encoder layer.

### 1.2.1.1. Pre-processing

The input sequence is passed through a series of pre-processing stages to get it ready for encoding. Figure 1.3 illustrates the three pre-processing stages involved in our neural machine translation example– tokenization, word embedding and positional encoding. Note that these stages are essential in the NLP applications for which the original Transformer model was designed. Applications in other fields such as computer vision would require distinct types of pre-processing.

### 1.2.1.1.1. Tokenization

The first pre-processing step is known as tokenization, where the input text is broken up into individual words that are referred to as *tokens*. The term token is used to refer to any general form of input and could be a word in NLP or a block of pixels in a vision application. The collection of input tokens forms a set, which by definition, has no notion of order. This means that any permutation of the words

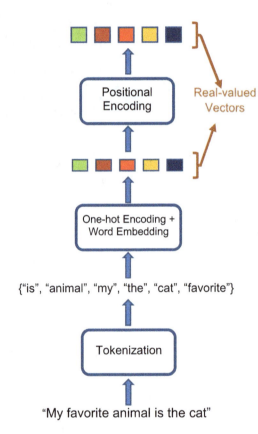

**Figure 1.3** Encoder Pre-processing Stages.

would produce the same set of tokens. The self-attention mechanism used in the encoder is agnostic to the order of the tokens. However, since the relative positions of words play a key role in natural language understanding, this information is inserted later on in the pre-processing chain.

## 1.2.1.1.2. Word Embeddings

The next step is to represent these tokens by numbers that can be understood by a computer. The simplest way to do this would be to create a sizeable dictionary of alphabetically sorted words, and then represent each input word by its index into the dictionary. Another similar idea is to create a vector of zeros of the size of the dictionary and place a 1 value in the vector at the index of the word in the dictionary. The latter approach is known as *one-hot encoding*.

While both these ideas solve the representation problem, they do not provide a way to relate similar words. Each word is treated as a completely independent entity with no relationship to any other word in the dictionary. However, in natural languages, groups of words are related in a variety of ways - they describe a common type of object, a common behavior etc. For example, the words cat and dog are closely related since both represent animals. Such a correlation should ideally manifest itself in similar representations for these words. Intuitively, the "distance" between the representations of the words cat and dog should be smaller than that between the representations of any of these words and that of some unrelated word such as bicycle. The vocabulary indexing and one-hot representations of words do not have the ability to capture such relationships. Also note that in the one-hot representation, each word lies at one of the edges of an $D$-dimensional unit hypercube, where $D$ is the size of the dictionary. This makes such a representation very inefficient as well (a single 1 with $D-1$ zeros for every word in a dictionary of size $D$ words). In our example task, if cat is at index 275 in the input English dictionary of size of 10000, it is represented by a 10000-dimensional vector with a value of 1 at index 275 and zeros everywhere else.

However, one-hot encoding still forms the first processing stage on the path to generating a suitable word representation. Each input token is converted to its one-hot representation based on a fixed input dictionary that is selected based on the application. The one-hot representation is then transformed into one that embeds some implicit information about each word. This is achieved in NLP applications by a process known as *word embedding* whereby the input one-hot vector (say $\vec{y}$) is projected using a learned embedding matrix (say $\mathbf{E}$) to generate a continuous-valued vector (say $\vec{x}$) that contains some language context for the word. Then we have,

$$\vec{x} = \vec{y}\mathbf{E}$$

In general, a projection is an operation that modifies the co-ordinate system (or representation subspace) of the input vector. The transformed co-ordinate system usually has fewer dimensions, and the projected vector is an altered representation of the input data that better suits a particular application. The operation involves the multiplication of the input vector by a matrix, known as a *projection matrix*, which is designed specifically for a certain task.

In the specific case of the Transformer, the output vector $\vec{x}$ is known as a *word embedding* and has a more compact representation (with fewer dimensions) when compared to the input vector $\vec{y}$. For example, $\vec{y}$ could have a size of 10,000 (when one-hot representation is used with 10,000 words in the source dictionary) whereas the embedding vector $\vec{x}$ would typically have a much smaller size (specifically, it is 512 in the original paper [1]). More importantly, this operation results in a structured representation where groups of embeddings that represent words with similar meanings are bunched together in the 512-dimension representation space. Note that the size of the embedding matrix $\mathbf{E}$ in this case is 10,000×512 (that is, $\mathbf{E} \in \mathbb{R}^{10,000 \times 512}$).

In the NLP realm, the one-hot representation of a word is referred to as a *local representation* and the embedding is known as a *distributed representation*. Note that the context provided by the word embeddings are representative of the general language and are independent of the actual piece of input text. The embedding matrix is learned during training using a large corpus of text which typically should not contain the data that is used at inference time.

Since an embedding has a smaller size when compared to that of the input dictionary, it forms a more efficient representation in addition to capturing the dependencies present in the language. Pre-trained word embeddings for the English language, such as Glove and Word2vec, are publicly available and are used for certain common NLP tasks. However, in the Transformer model, the embedding matrix is learned during training, to optimize the distributed representation to the specific task at hand.

### 1.2.1.1.3. Positional Encoding

Due to the tokenization step at the beginning of the processing chain, the word embeddings do not contain any information about the order of the words in the input text. However, in languages, the position of a word in a piece of text plays a key role in making complete sense of the text. Therefore, some indication of the order of each word needs to be added to each word embedding. This process, known as *positional encoding*, is the last stage of sequence pre-processing in the encoder half of the Transformer model. In the original paper, positional encoding was achieved by simply creating a positional vector for each word embedding (based on its index in the input sequence) and adding together the two vectors. Since both these vectors are made up of continuous values, the result is also a continuous-valued vector.

Each positional encoding vector has the same size ($d_{model} = 512$) as the word embeddings to ensure that the vectors can be summed. The position vectors are generated using two sinusoidal functions (sine and cosine, for the even and odd dimension indices respectively) each of which takes in the word index and the dimension index as input parameters. Specifically, the position encoding functions are given by:

$$PE(word_{idx}, dim_{even}) = sin\left(\frac{word_{idx}}{10000^{\frac{dim_{even}}{d_{model}}}}\right),$$

$$PE(word_{idx}, dim_{odd}) = cos\left(\frac{word\_idx}{10000^{\frac{dim_{odd}-1}{d_{model}}}}\right)$$

where $word_{idx}$ is the index of the word in the sequence, $dim_{even} \in \{0,2,4,...,d_{model}-2\}$ and $dim_{odd} \in \{1,3,5,...,d_{model}-1\}$ are the vector dimension indices. Each dimension of the positional encoding vector is encoded as a unique combination of sinusoidal frequency and phase. The idea behind using sinusoidal positional encodings rather than absolute position values is that the former can be extended and generalized to input sequences of any length. This approach decorrelates the lengths of the sequences used during training from those that the Transformer could encounter during inference. The addition of positional information is the last pre-processing stage in the generation of the input embeddings, which are then fed to the first encoder layer in the stack.

### 1.2.1.2. Encoder Architecture

A Transformer encoder layer (figure 1.2) consists of a multi-head self-attention sub-layer, a feed-forward sub-layer, residual connections and layer normalization blocks. The structure and function of each sub-layer are described in the following sections.

### 1.2.1.2.1. Self-Attention Mechanism

Attention can be thought of as memory through time, and it is the mechanism that assigns weights to neighboring words based on how much they enhance the meaning of a word of interest. The mechanism is analogous to how humans place different degrees of emphasis on different words when reading a piece of text. Certain words are more important in conveying the central idea of the piece, while a few others could be ignored without changing the reader's understanding. The importance of a word lies intuitively in the context that it provides to other words in the piece of text. The attention mechanism in the Transformer architecture helps in quantifying such a context for each embedding from the input sequence. It is a means to capture the level of dependency between pairs of embeddings, and to summarize the influence that an embedding might have on all of the other embeddings in the input sequence.

As a simple illustration of why the self-attention mechanism is effective, we revisit the example of translating the English sentence My favorite animal is the cat to French. The expected translation is Mon animal préféré est le chat. The mapping between the corresponding words (or word translations) in the two sentences is shown below.

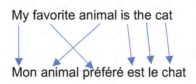

Notice how the relative positions of the corresponding words are different in the input and output sequences even in this simple example. This happens because of the differences in the grammatical structures of languages. In this case, the adjective in the French sentence follows the noun, whereas the order is reversed in the English sentence. Therefore, simply stringing together the translations of the words in the input sequence will not produce a correct translated sequence. The Transformer model learns to pay "attention" to the appropriate parts of the input sequence as it constructs the output sequence, and the self-attention mechanism is what enables it to do so. The attention mechanism in general equips the Transformer model to learn the nuances and unique grammatical constructs of languages.

The concepts of query, key and value that were discussed in section 1.1.2 lie at the core of the attention mechanism. In this context, the query for an input token corresponds to a transformed version of its embedding vector, the keys correspond to the (differently) transformed embeddings of all the tokens in the input sequence and the value corresponds to a third transformed version of the current token's embedding. Since the query, key and value vectors are derived from the same sequence of tokens, this flavor of the attention mechanism is referred to as *self-attention*.

The paper by Vaswani et al. gave us the following formula for attention, where **Q**, **K** and **V** are the matrices formed by stacking together all the query, key and value vectors, respectively, of the tokens in the input sequence.

$$Attention(\mathbf{Q}, \mathbf{K}, \mathbf{V}) = Softmax\left(\frac{\mathbf{Q}\mathbf{K}^\mathbf{T}}{\sqrt{L_Q}}\right)\mathbf{V}$$

We will derive this formula here from first principles. The first step in computing self-attention is to generate the query, key and value vectors for each input embedding. They are generated by projecting each input embedding using three different matrices, each of which is learned during training.

Consider the case when the input sequence contains $N$ tokens, which are used to generate $N$ embeddings ($N = 6$ in our example translation task). A single input embedding $\vec{x}_i$ of size $L_E (= 512$ in the original design) is modified into a query vector $\vec{q}_i$ of size $L_Q$ using the projection matrix $\mathbf{W_Q}$. Similarly, $\vec{x}_i$ is transformed into a key vector $\vec{k}_i$ (with $L_K$ components) and value vector $\vec{v}_i$ (with $L_V$ components) using the projection matrices $\mathbf{W_K}$ and $\mathbf{W_V}$ respectively. These projections are applied to every input embedding vector $\vec{x}_i, 0 \leq i \leq N - 1$. In the Transformer architecture, the projection matrices $\mathbf{W_Q}$, $\mathbf{W_K}$ and $\mathbf{W_V}$ are learned independently during training. We then have,

$$\vec{q}_i = \vec{x}_i \mathbf{W_Q}; \ \vec{k}_i = \vec{x}_i \mathbf{W_K}; \ \vec{v}_i = \vec{x}_i \mathbf{W_V}.$$

Attention is a measure of correlation and can be computed in various ways. The original Transformer paper used the scaled dot-product attention as the mechanism of choice. As discussed in section 1.1.3, the dot-product is used to quantify the similarity between two continuous-valued vectors. In the context of attention, it is used to quantify the relevance between the query and key vectors.

Dot-products are computed between each query vector $\vec{q}_i$ and the set of key vectors $\vec{k}_j$, $0 \leq j \leq N-1$, and the array of dot-products is scaled by $\sqrt{L_Q}$, where $L_Q$ is the size of the query vector. The scaled dot-product vector is passed to a softmax function that generates an output array of real values in the range $(0,1)$. The final attention vector for embedding $i$ is calculated as follows.

$$\vec{s}_i = Softmax\left(\frac{\left[\vec{q}_i\vec{k}_0^T, \vec{q}_i\vec{k}_1^T, \ldots, \vec{q}_i\vec{k}_{N-1}^T\right]}{\sqrt{L_Q}}\right)$$

Since $\vec{q}_i$ is a $1 \times L_Q$ vector and $\vec{k}_j^T$ is a $L_K \times 1$ vector, the dot-product operation makes it necessary for $L_K$ to be equal to $L_Q$. This also means that the learned projection matrices $\mathbf{W_Q}$ and $\mathbf{W_K}$ have identical dimensions. Note that each dot product results in a scalar value and the division by $\sqrt{L_Q}$ ensures that the inputs to the softmax function do not take on very large values. This ensures that the softmax function operates in a high-gradient region and is seen to help in speeding up the training of the model. The vector of the $N$ scaled dot-products is passed through a softmax activation function to yield a vector $\vec{s}_i$, one for each input embedding.

The symbol $s_{i,j}$ is used to indicate the value of the $j^{th}$ component of the vector $\vec{s}_i$ and it denotes the *attention weight* that the input embedding at index $i$ places on the embedding at index $j$. The $s_{i,j}$ values are used to scale the respective value vectors $\vec{v}_j$ to generate the output attention vector for the current location $i$. Mathematically, the attention vector is generated as a weighted sum of value vectors.

$$\vec{a}_i = \sum_{j=0}^{N-1} s_{i,j}\vec{v}_j$$

The attention vector $\vec{a}_i$ has a size of $L_V$ since it is a linear combination of the value vectors of that size. One such vector is computed for each input embedding (for a total of $N$ vectors). These vectors serve as the input embeddings to the next encoder in the stack. While it is not necessary for the value vectors to be of the same size as the query and key vectors, enforcing this condition simplifies the architecture because it keeps the size of the input embeddings constant throughout the entire encoder stack.

The above computation can be parallelized over all of the input embeddings using matrix operations in order to save on compute time. Let $\mathbf{X}$ be the matrix that is formed by stacking together the $N$ input embeddings with resulting dimensions of $N \times L_E$.

$$X = \begin{bmatrix} \vec{x}_0 \\ \vec{x}_1 \\ \vdots \\ \vec{x}_{N-1} \end{bmatrix}$$

The matrix of all the queries can be computed in a single matrix operation as $\mathbf{Q} = \mathbf{X}\mathbf{W_Q}$, where the matrix $\mathbf{W_Q} \in \mathbb{R}^{L_E \times L_Q}$ and the matrix $\mathbf{Q} \in \mathbb{R}^{N \times L_Q}$.

$$\mathbf{Q} = \mathbf{X}\mathbf{W_Q} = \begin{bmatrix} \vec{q}_0 \\ \vec{q}_1 \\ \vdots \\ \vec{q}_{N-1} \end{bmatrix}$$

The matrix of all the keys is computed as $\mathbf{K} = \mathbf{X}\mathbf{W_K}$, where $\mathbf{W_K} \in \mathbb{R}^{L_E \times L_Q}$ and $\mathbf{K} \in \mathbb{R}^{N \times L_Q}$.

$$\mathbf{K} = \mathbf{X}\mathbf{W_K} = \begin{bmatrix} \vec{k}_0 \\ \vec{k}_1 \\ \vdots \\ \vec{k}_{N-1} \end{bmatrix}$$

The matrix of all the value vectors is computed as $\mathbf{V} = \mathbf{X}\mathbf{W_V}$, where $\mathbf{W_V} \in \mathbb{R}^{L_E \times L_V}$ and $\mathbf{V} \in \mathbb{R}^{N \times L_V}$.

$$\mathbf{V} = \mathbf{X}\mathbf{W_V} = \begin{bmatrix} \vec{v}_0 \\ \vec{v}_1 \\ \vdots \\ \vec{v}_{N-1} \end{bmatrix}$$

The attention values for every pair of input embeddings can also be computed using a single matrix multiplication operation as shown in eq. (1). The operation results in a matrix $\mathbf{D}$ that contains all of the $N \times N$ dot-product results. Note that $\mathbf{D}$ is a matrix of scaler values that quantify the pair-wise attention values between the input embeddings, and since attention is not a commutative operation, $\mathbf{D}$ is *not* a symmetric matrix.

$$\mathbf{D} = \mathbf{Q}\mathbf{K^T} = \begin{bmatrix} \vec{q}_0 \\ \vec{q}_1 \\ \vdots \\ \vec{q}_{N-1} \end{bmatrix} \begin{bmatrix} \vec{k}_0^T & \vec{k}_1^T & \dots & \vec{k}_{N-1}^T \end{bmatrix} = \begin{bmatrix} \vec{q}_0\vec{k}_0^T & \cdots & \vec{q}_0\vec{k}_{N-1}^T \\ \vdots & \ddots & \vdots \\ \vec{q}_{N-1}\vec{k}_0^T & \cdots & \vec{q}_{N-1}\vec{k}_{N-1}^T \end{bmatrix}$$

$$= \begin{bmatrix} d_{0,0} & \cdots & d_{0,N-1} \\ \vdots & \ddots & \vdots \\ d_{N-1,0} & \cdots & d_{N-1,N-1} \end{bmatrix} \qquad \dots (1)$$

The matrix $\mathbf{D}$ is scaled by the quantity $\sqrt{L_Q}$ and passed through a softmax function that operates on *one row of the matrix at a time* to generate another $N \times N$ matrix $\mathbf{S}$ of scaling coefficients. Note that every entry in $\mathbf{S}$ has a value between 0 and 1.

$$\mathbf{S} = Softmax\left(\frac{\mathbf{D}}{\sqrt{L_Q}}\right) = \begin{bmatrix} Softmax\left(\frac{d_{0,0}}{\sqrt{L_Q}}, \frac{d_{0,1}}{\sqrt{L_Q}}, \dots, \frac{d_{0,N-1}}{\sqrt{L_Q}}\right) \\ Softmax\left(\frac{d_{1,0}}{\sqrt{L_Q}}, \frac{d_{1,1}}{\sqrt{L_Q}}, \dots, \frac{d_{1,N-1}}{\sqrt{L_Q}}\right) \\ \vdots \\ Softmax\left(\frac{d_{N-1,0}}{\sqrt{L_Q}}, \frac{d_{N-1,1}}{\sqrt{L_Q}}, \dots, \frac{d_{N-1,N-1}}{\sqrt{L_Q}}\right) \end{bmatrix}$$

$$= \begin{bmatrix} s_{0,0} & \cdots & s_{0,N-1} \\ \vdots & \ddots & \vdots \\ s_{N-1,0} & \cdots & s_{N-1,N-1} \end{bmatrix} \quad \dots (2)$$

Each row of coefficients from $\mathbf{S}$ is used to scale all of the value vectors to generate one attention vector output. Together, an attention matrix $\mathbf{A} \in \mathbb{R}^{N \times L_V}$ is generated using the matrices $\mathbf{S}$ and $\mathbf{V}$ as shown in equation (3).

$$\mathbf{A} = \mathbf{SV} = \begin{bmatrix} s_{0,0} & \cdots & s_{0,N-1} \\ \vdots & \ddots & \vdots \\ s_{N-1,0} & \cdots & s_{N-1,N-1} \end{bmatrix} \begin{bmatrix} \vec{v}_0 \\ \vec{v}_1 \\ \vdots \\ \vec{v}_{N-1} \end{bmatrix}$$

$$= \begin{bmatrix} s_{0,0}\vec{v}_0 + s_{0,1}\vec{v}_1 + \cdots + s_{0,N-1}\vec{v}_{N-1} \\ s_{1,0}\vec{v}_0 + s_{1,1}\vec{v}_1 + \cdots + s_{1,N-1}\vec{v}_{N-1} \\ \vdots \\ s_{N-1,0}\vec{v}_0 + s_{N-1,1}\vec{v}_1 + \cdots + s_{N-1,N-1}\vec{v}_{N-1} \end{bmatrix} = \begin{bmatrix} \vec{a}_0 \\ \vec{a}_1 \\ \vdots \\ \vec{a}_{N-1} \end{bmatrix} \quad \dots (3)$$

Combining equations (1), (2) and (3), we arrive at the original equation for attention.

$$Attention(\mathbf{Q}, \mathbf{K}, \mathbf{V}) = Softmax\left(\frac{\mathbf{QK^T}}{\sqrt{L_Q}}\right)\mathbf{V}$$

## 1.2.1.2.2. Multi-head Attention

The Transformer architecture further refines the self-attention layer by adding a mechanism called *multi-head attention.* This improves the performance of the attention layer by allowing the model to gather information on several different attributes of the input sequence. This is also one way of preventing the attention weights for each input embedding from being dominated by a single embedding (usually itself).

A *head* refers to one attention block that produces a sequence of attention vectors as discussed earlier, and each attention head uses an independent set of projection matrices. The operations performed within one attention head in the encoder to generate one attention vector, for the machine translation example with six input tokens, are illustrated in figure 1.4. The original Transformer consists of eight attention heads in each encoder block and therefore uses eight sets of query/key/value weight matrices ($\mathbf{W_Q^i}$, $\mathbf{W_K^i}$ and $\mathbf{W_V^i}$ in figure 1.4). Each of these matrices is randomly initialized and learned during training.

The use of the multiple attention heads enables the model to look at different parts of the input independently and contributes to the superior performance of Transformers over CNNs. The intuition behind using multiple heads is that each head can focus on gathering information about one of these basic attributes – "who," "what," "where," "when", "why", "how", singular/plural, male/female etc. The Transformer is able to build a rich context for every token in the input sequence by allowing each head to focus on a specific type of dependency. A single head might not be successful in capturing all of these dependencies by itself.

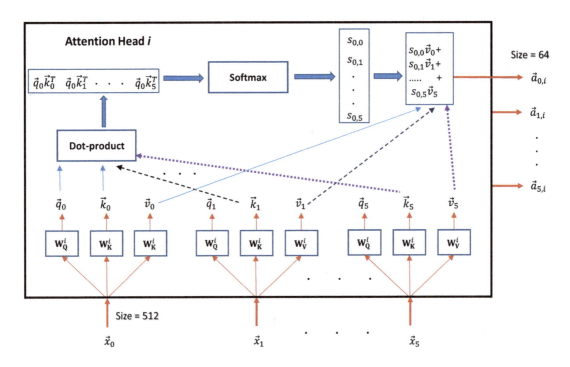

**Figure 1.4** Operations to Generate the Attention Vector for Input Embedding $\vec{x}_0$ ($N = 6$) in one Attention Head.

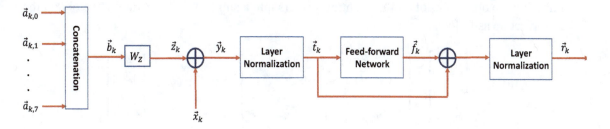

**Figure 1.5** Post-processing of Attention Vectors for Input Embedding $\vec{x}_k$.

Each attention head generates one attention vector for every input embedding, and the vectors are combined into a single embedding that can be used for further processing. The sequence of operations performed in the rest of the encoder layer, on the outputs of the eight attention heads for each input embedding, are illustrated in figure 1.5. Expanding on the notations used above, let $\vec{a}_{k,h}$ denote the attention vector generated by attention head $h$ for the $k^{\text{th}}$ input embedding. The corresponding output attention vectors for this embedding from the 8 attention heads are simply concatenated into a single vector $\vec{b}_k$ as follows.

$$\vec{b}_k =< \vec{a}_{k,0}\vec{a}_{k,1} \ldots \vec{a}_{k,7} >.$$

The resulting vector $\vec{b}_k$ now has a size that is eight times that of the candidate attention vectors. However, in order to enable the residual connections (see section 1.2.1.2.3) around the attention layer, it is essential that the input and output embeddings have the same number of components. This is enforced by limiting the size of each individual attention vector $\vec{a}_{k,h}$ to an eighth of the size of an input embedding vector. Since the original paper used an embedding size ($L_E$) of 512 elements, each attention vector $\vec{a}_{k,h}$ has $\frac{512}{8} = 64$ components. Therefore, each concatenated vector $\vec{b}_k$ ends up with the required size of 512 components.

As noted in section 1.2.1.2.1, each attention vector has the same size as the value vectors. Therefore, in the original Transformer, each attention head generates value vectors with 64 components ($L_V = 64$). While the query and key vectors could have a different size ($L_Q = L_K$ always), practical implementations use $L_Q = L_K = 64$. Each attention head works independently, and all the attention heads can be run in parallel at the same time. This can be leveraged to greatly increase the speed of both the training and inference of the network.

Each concatenated attention vector $\vec{b}_k$ is again projected using another learnable projection matrix $\mathbf{W_z}$ to generate the final processed feature vector $\vec{z}_k$ for $0 \le k \le N - 1$. Note that we need $\vec{z}_k$ to be a 512-dimensional vector since it is combined with its corresponding input embedding via a residual connection.

Combining the operations of all the attention vectors into a single matrix operation, we obtain the feature vectors as follows:

$$\mathbf{B} = \begin{bmatrix} \vec{b}_0 \\ \vec{b}_1 \\ \vdots \\ \vec{b}_{N-1} \end{bmatrix} = \begin{bmatrix} < \vec{a}_{0,0}\,\vec{a}_{0,1} \cdots \vec{a}_{0,7} > \\ < \vec{a}_{1,0}\,\vec{a}_{1,1} \cdots \vec{a}_{1,7} > \\ \vdots \\ < \vec{a}_{N-1,0}\,\vec{a}_{N-1,1} \cdots \vec{a}_{N-1,7} > \end{bmatrix} ; \quad \mathbf{Z} = \mathbf{BW_z} = \begin{bmatrix} \vec{z}_0 \\ \vec{z}_1 \\ \vdots \\ \vec{z}_{N-1} \end{bmatrix}$$

A subtle point to note is that, theoretically, the $\vec{b}_i$ vectors above could potentially have had any number of components (and not necessarily 512) since the dimensions of the $\mathbf{W_z}$ matrix could have been modified to compensate for the change. However, limiting the size of the concatenated vectors helps in reducing the computational complexity of the encoder.

### 1.2.1.2.3. Residual Connections and Layer Normalization

Another important feature of the Transformer architecture is the residual connection around each of the attention blocks. A residual connection, also known as a skip connection, is a means for the model to combine the information carried by the input embeddings of the multi-head attention block with additional information that might have been gained during the attention computation process. In the NLP realm, this is akin to combining high-level language information with lower-level sequence-specific information.

As shown in figure 1.5, the residual connection is implemented as the element-wise addition of the corresponding input vectors to, and the output vectors from, the attention sub-layer. This is possible because these vectors are designed to have the same number of components. Following the notation used above, if the input embeddings are denoted by $\vec{x}_i$ and the output embeddings are denoted by $\vec{z}_i$, we have the combined vector $\vec{y}_i = \vec{x}_i + \vec{z}_i$ for $0 \le i \le N - 1$. The residual connections are intended to improve performance in two ways – combine the understanding of the sequence at a coarse level (before attention computation) with the understanding gathered from the attention computation and pass along the positional encoding information through the successive encoders.

Layer normalization is a practice used in machine learning to limit the range of values in a feature vector. It is aimed at preventing the mean and the standard deviation of the features from shifting around in a wide range, since that could make the training process unstable and slow. The normalization operation is applied across the outputs of all the nodes in a neural network layer to generate a feature vector with a mean value of zero mean and standard deviation of unity. In the Transformer model, normalization is applied to each 512-dimensional vector $\vec{y}_i$, at the output of the residual connection layer. The first step is to compute the mean $\mu_i$ and the standard deviation $\sigma_i$ of the components.

$$\mu_i = \frac{1}{512} \sum_{j=1}^{512} \vec{y}_{i,j}$$

$$\sigma_i = \sqrt{\frac{1}{512} \sum_{j=1}^{512} \left(\vec{y}_{i,j} - \mu_i\right)^2}$$

The next step is to normalize the components of the vector to yield a vector with mean zero and standard deviation of one. The normalized vector is indicated by $\vec{y}_i^{norm}$.

$$\vec{y}_i^{norm} = \frac{\vec{y}_i - \mu_i}{\sigma_i}$$

The normalized vector is then modified to one whose components have a mean $\Delta$ and a standard deviation $\lambda$. These parameters are learned during training and are therefore tuned to help yield the best performance for the particular application. The final scaled and shifted vector is denoted by $\vec{t}_i$ and is given by

$$\vec{t}_i = \lambda \vec{y}_i^{norm} + \Delta$$

The normalization process is repeated for every input embedding $\vec{x}_i$ for $0 \leq i \leq N - 1$. The values of the parameters $\Delta$ and $\lambda$ are fixed across all of the vectors. Note that the normalization process does not change the dimensions of the vectors.

## 1.2.1.2.4. Feed-forward Network (FFN)

The position-wise FFN is a fully-connected neural network that processes the layer-normalized embeddings in parallel. The term "position-wise" implies that each embedding is independently passed through the network, which treats each component of an input vector as an independent data point at one of its input nodes. This network, shown in figure 1.6, consumes the outputs $\vec{t}_i$ that are generated by the layer normalization block as discussed in the previous section. The input and output layers of the FFN are each made up of 512 nodes whereas the hidden layer consists of 2048 nodes. The network applies the ReLU activation function to the feature vector in the hidden layer.

Activation functions in a neural network introduce non-linearities in the data path and enable the network to learn complex functions during the training process. The ReLU is the simplest such function, and it clamps the value of the output to zero if the input value is negative but allows all the non-negative inputs to pass through with no change. In the Transformer FFN, the ReLU function is applied independently to each of the 2048 components of the feature vector in the hidden layer in order to zero out negative feature values. While this operation enables the remaining blocks to operate on unsigned data, it also leads to the loss of some information. This

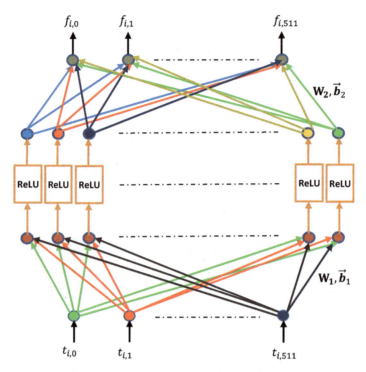

**Figure 1.6** Position-wise Feed-forward Network.

is the intuition behind increasing the dimensionality of the data in the hidden layer before the ReLU activation is applied. The output layer has to reduce the size of the embedding because the residual connection around the FFN (see figure 1.5) requires that the output vector of the FFN is of the same size as the input vector.

Letting $\vec{t}_i$ be the output of the self-attention sub-layer, the operation of the FFN can be summarized as

$$FFN(\vec{t}_i) = \vec{f}_i = ReLU(\vec{t}_i\mathbf{W_1} + \vec{b}_1)\mathbf{W_2} + \vec{b}_2 = \max\left(\vec{\mathbf{0}}, (\vec{t}_i\mathbf{W_1} + \vec{b}_1)\right)\mathbf{W_2} + \vec{b}_2, 0 \leq i \leq N\text{-}1.$$

The vector zero vector $\vec{\mathbf{0}}$ above is of size $1\times2048$ and is used to indicate that the ReLU function operates independently on each component of the vector result $(\vec{t}_i\mathbf{W_1} + \vec{b}_1)$ of the first layer. The weight matrices $\mathbf{W_1}$ and $\mathbf{W_2}$, and the bias vectors $\vec{b}_1$ and $\vec{b}_2$ are learned during training, and the same weights and biases are applied to all the embeddings in each layer.

The output vector from the FFN is combined with the corresponding input vector through a residual connection and layer-normalized just like in the case of the attention sub-layer described above. Referring to figure 1.5, we have the final output embeddings of the encoder layer as $\vec{r}_i =$

$LN(\vec{f_i} + \vec{t_i})$ for $0 \le i \le N - 1$. The normalized embeddings become the outputs of the current encoder block and are used as inputs to the next encoder block in the stack.

### 1.2.1.3. Encoder Stack Operation

The Transformer architecture consists of a stack of six identical encoder layers. However, they do not share weights and each encoder uses its own learnable projection matrices $\mathbf{W_Q}$, $\mathbf{W_K}$ and $\mathbf{W_V}$. Note that the initial embedding and positional encoding steps are applied solely to the inputs of the first encoder block. Each of the remaining five encoders simply uses the output embeddings from the previous encoder. The design of the encoders is simplified by ensuring that the input and output vectors have a fixed dimension of 512 components. The intuition behind using multiple encoders seems to be that each encoder builds upon the learnings of all the previous encoders and adds some incremental information of its own to the embeddings.

The embeddings produced by the last encoder in the stack are further processed to generate key and value vectors for use by the decoder. Each of the output embeddings is projected using learnable matrices $\mathbf{W_{EK}}$ and $\mathbf{W_{EV}}$, respectively, to generate a key vector $\vec{k_i^E} = \vec{r_i}\mathbf{W_{EK}}$ and a value vector $\vec{v_i^E} = \vec{r_i}\mathbf{W_{EV}}$ for $0 \le i \le N - 1$. These vectors are computed in parallel using a single matrix operation to yield an encoder value matrix $\mathbf{V}_{enc} \in \mathbb{R}^{N \times 512}$ and an encoder key matrix $\mathbf{K}_{enc} \in \mathbb{R}^{N \times 512}$ .

In our simple machine translation example, the input English sentence my favorite animal is the cat is now represented by a set of six key vectors and a set of six value vectors. As discussed later in this document, these key and value vectors are used in the computation of the encoder-decoder cross-attention where the query vectors are generated by the decoder. The intuition here is that these key and value vectors capture the dependencies between the input tokens at a global level, which is critical to the overall understanding of the sequence. The decoder then has access to all of this global information at every decoding time step.

## 1.2.2. Decoder Stack

Figure 1.7 shows the data flow within and between the encoder and the decoder stacks. The encoder stack processes the entire input sequence at once and each successive encoder bubbles up its results to the next encoder in the stack. The output embeddings of the last encoder are then transformed into a matrix of key vectors $\mathbf{K}_{enc}$ and a matrix of value vectors $\mathbf{V}_{enc}$. These vectors are used by each decoder in its "encoder-decoder attention" layer which helps the decoder focus on appropriate tokens in the input sequence. The decoder stack consists of six identical decoder layers that generate output embeddings with identical dimensions.

One new token in the output sequence is generated at every time step of the decoding phase. This token is converted to an embedding and positionally encoded in a manner similar to how tokens

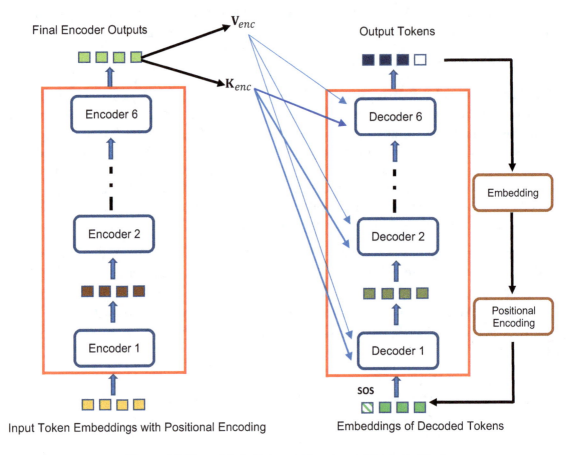

**Figure 1.7** Flow of Data Between Encoder and Decoder Stacks.

are pre-processed at the input to the encoder stack. At every decoding time step, all the embeddings that have been decoded so far are fed to the decoder stack. The individual decoders generate a sequence of embeddings and bubble them up through the stack. The number of embeddings at the output of a decoder layer is equal to the number of embeddings at its input. Since this number increases by one at each time step (due to a new output token that is pre-processed and fed to the decoder stack), each decoder layer generates an additional embedding at every time step. The details of the decoding operation are explained in the sections to follow.

At every time step, the decoder stack receives two sets of inputs – the value and key vectors from the encoder and the embedded vectors of all of the previously decoded tokens. Each decoder layer consists of a masked attention sub-layer, a cross attention sub-layer, a feed-forward network, normalization layers and residual connections. The following sections describe the sub-layers in the decoder architecture, and then use our machine translation example to illustrate the operations of the decoder stack.

## 1.2.2.1. Pre-processing

The decoder stack operates in an auto-regressive manner, which means that it consumes the output tokens that it has already generated in order to generate the next output token. The output token could be a word from a dictionary or a block of pixels in an image. The tokens need to be transformed into a form that the decoder can consume. The position of each token in the output sequence could also convey important information to the decoder. This situation is identical to that at the input of the encoder stack. Therefore, the decoded tokens are passed through the same pre-processing stages that are employed on the encoder side – embedding and positional encoding. Note that the order of tokens is important to the decoder stack because each decoder consists of a masked self-attention layer (see section 1.2.2.2.1 below). The order did not matter on the encoder side because the entire input sequence was processed at once.

The embedding matrix is learned during network training, and in some implementations, shares weights with the embedding matrix used for the encoder stack. The positional encoding method is identical to that of the encoder and uses the sine and cosine signals to encode the index of the token. Pre-processing is applied to the new tokens once before they are fed to the first decoder in the stack. Each subsequent decoder consumes the embeddings that have been generated by the previous decoder.

## 1.2.2.2. Decoder Architecture

A decoder layer in the Transformer (figure 1.2) contains all of the sub-layers that make up the encoder layer with an additional cross-attention sub-layer. The multi-head self-attention sub-layer, however, operates in a slightly different manner in the decoder. The architecture of the sub-layers in the decoder are discussed in the following sections.

## 1.2.2.2.1. Masked Self-attention

The first decoder in the stack consumes the embeddings of the decoded tokens directly, whereas subsequent decoders consume the output embeddings from the previous decoder in the stack. Each decoder uses a modified version of the multi-head self-attention layer that is used in the encoder. The self-attention computation at any embedding position is performed using only those embeddings that have already been decoded. In other words, the attention computation is causal, and at *every* position, all the future token positions in the output sequence are "masked off." Hence this type of attention computation is known as *masked self-attention*. Figure 1.8 illustrates the difference in the operations of the regular attention and the masked attention layers for a hypothetical sequence with just four embeddings. Note that since this is also a self-attention layer, the queries, keys and values are generated from the same sequence of embeddings.

The concept of masked self-attention originates from the process used to train the decoder stack for language tasks. The Transformer decoders are usually trained in such cases using techniques

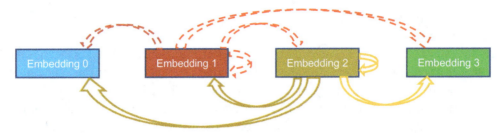

(a) **Regular Self-attention** – Pair-wise attention computations are shown for input embeddings at positions 1 and 2. All the input embeddings are used.

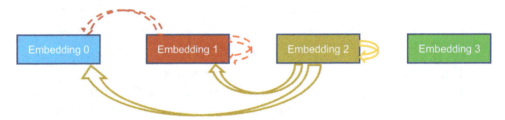

(b) **Masked Self-attention** – Pair-wise attention computations are shown for input embeddings at positions 1 and 2. Only those embeddings that have appeared earlier in the sequence are used.

**Figure 1.8** Flavors of Attention Mechanism in the Transformer Architecture ($N = 4$).

such as next-word or next-sentence prediction. This approach iteratively trains the decoder to predict the next word in the target sequence given the encoded input sequence and the current version of the decoded target sequence. At every training iteration, the performance of the decoder stack is evaluated on how accurately it is able to perform this prediction, by comparing the predicted word with the actual word in the training text. There is a problem with this approach, however, since during training, the decoder stack has access to the entire target sequence which includes the word that it is supposed to predict. Therefore, the decoders could "learn to cheat" during training and just copy the relevant word from the training sequence. If this were allowed, the decoder stack would fail to learn anything of value and the model's performance at inference time would be very poor. It is therefore essential that the decoders are prevented from looking ahead at the future words in the training text. This is achieved by masking off the non-causal portions of the training text during attention computation and forcing the decoders to learn to actually predict the next word. Since the decoders are trained in this fashion, the same mechanism carries over to model inference as well, even though the decoders no longer have access to the non-causal tokens.

The masked self-attention layer is identical in design to the regular attention layer in the encoder (section 1.2.1.2.1), and masking is achieved by setting to $-\infty$ the appropriate locations of the input matrix to the softmax function. Note that this causes the corresponding outputs of the softmax function to approach zero, and therefore the corresponding value vectors to be scaled to zero. This operation is implemented using a mask matrix as shown in the equation below, where **M** is a $t \times t$ matrix which is generated at decoding time step $t$. Since $t$ target tokens have been generated so far, the matrix $\mathbf{QK}^T$ also has a size of $t \times t$. All the entries above the diagonal in **M** are set to $-\infty$ (in theory, and a large negative number in practice) and the remaining entries are set to zero. The zero-valued entries in **M** ensure that the valid attention computations are not affected, and the other entries ensure that the decoder only attends to the past target tokens.

$$\mathbf{M}_{t \times t} = \begin{bmatrix} 0 & -\infty & \cdots & \cdots & \cdots & -\infty \\ 0 & 0 & -\infty & \cdots & \cdots & -\infty \\ 0 & 0 & 0 & -\infty & \cdots & -\infty \\ \vdots & \cdots & \cdots & \ddots & \ddots & \vdots \\ & \cdots & \cdots & \cdots & 0 & -\infty \\ 0 & \cdots & \cdots & \cdots & 0 & 0 \end{bmatrix};$$

$$MaskedAttention(\mathbf{Q}, \mathbf{K}, \mathbf{V}) = Softmax\left(\frac{\mathbf{QK}^T}{\sqrt{L_Q}} + \mathbf{M}_{t \times t}\right)\mathbf{V}$$

The post-processing stage of the outputs of the attention heads is identical to that on the encoder side (figure 1.5). Each decoder layer consists of eight masked attention heads with each attention head producing output vectors that are one-eighth the size of the final attention vector. The process of combining the results of the attention heads is similar to that in the encoder. The results for the attention heads are concatenated and projected using another learned matrix to generate a single attention vector for each input embedding. The outputs of the masked-attention layer are added to the corresponding input vectors via a residual connection and the resulting vectors are layer-normalized.

## 1.2.2.2.2. Cross-attention

Each decoder uses a second variation of the attention mechanism in addition to masked self-attention. This is the encoder-decoder *cross-attention* sub-layer whose operation is similar to that of the multi-headed self-attention layer, with the difference being that it uses the keys and values directly from the output of the encoder stack. Figure 1.9 illustrates the operations that are performed in this sub-layer at any given decoding time step. The queries are still created from the embeddings generated by the previous decoder layer. The current layer uses just a single learnable projection matrix ($\mathbf{D}_Q^i$ in figure 1.9) to generate the queries for cross-attention computation since the key and value vectors from the encoder stack are not processed further inside any of the decoders. The attention computation uses all of the encoder's keys and values for each decoder query vector. Note that the attention vectors for the tokens from the previous timesteps need not be recomputed since their values cannot change once they are generated.

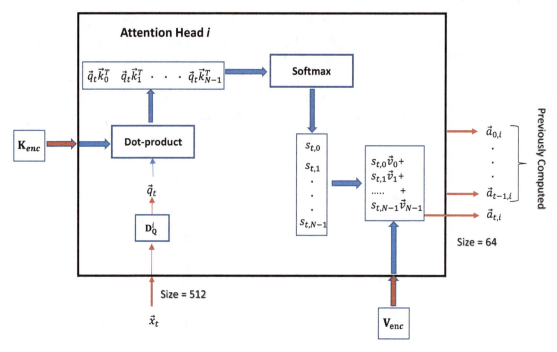

**Figure 1.9** Operations of a Cross-attention Head at Decoding Time Step $t$ ($N$ = number of input tokens at the encoder, $\vec{x}_t$ = newest input token at the decoder).

At each decoding step, every decoder layer applies the cross-attention mechanism using the queries built from the output of its own multi-head attention sub-layer and the key and value vectors from the encoded input sequence. This mechanism ensures that the decoders have the context of the entire input sequence as well as that of the current version of the output sequence to generate the most appropriate output token in the current decoding step.

Eight cross-attention heads are used in every decoder block. The attention vectors from these heads are concatenated and projected as described previously. The outputs of the cross-attention layer are again combined with the corresponding input vectors via a residual connection and the results are layer-normalized.

The remaining processing stages in the decoder (point-wise linear feed-forward layer, residual connection and layer normalization) are identical to the corresponding processing stages of the encoder shown in figure 1.5.

## 1.2.2.2.3. From Embeddings to Tokens

The first output embedding is produced by the decoder stack after the first decoding time step. In a naïve implementation, this embedding is generated by the decoder stack at every time step until all the target embeddings have been generated. The second output embedding is produced for the first time after the second time step and then at all the time steps until the end of the decoding operation. This pattern of output generation continues until the last embedding (usually an "end-of-sequence" or EOS embedding) is generated (just once) at the final time step. The number of target embeddings generated by the decoder stack increases by one at each time step. In an optimized implementation of the decoder, each new output embedding is generated just once, and the results of all the computations are cached and reused. This eliminates the wasted effort in recomputing the earlier output embeddings at every time step.

Irrespective of the implementation, the newest embedding at the output of the last decoder in the stack is used to generate the latest output token. This embedding is a representation of the output word (or token in general) in a 512-dimensional space and needs to be mapped to a word in the target dictionary. This is achieved by passing the embedding through a final linear layer followed by a softmax layer.

This operation, which is a process of multi-class classification, is illustrated in figure 1.10. The linear layer is a simple fully-connected classification neural network with no hidden layers and no

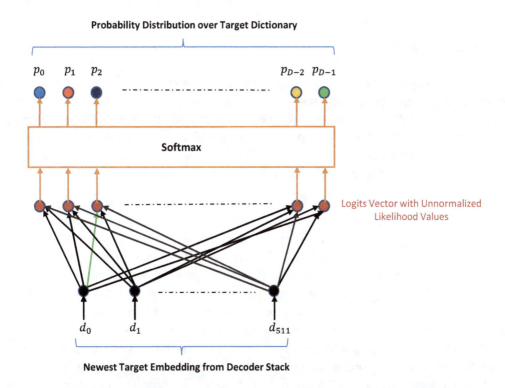

**Figure 1.10** Mapping of an Embedding to a Probability Distribution ($D$ is the number of words in the target dictionary).

non-linear activation function. It projects the 512-dimensional vector $\vec{d}_i$, produced by the decoder stack, into a larger vector called a *logits* vector. In general, the size of the logits vector is equal to the number of known classes and the logits vector is an ordered collection of un-normalized prediction scores for each known class. When the values of the logits vector are normalized, the resulting vector is a probability distribution over the various classes.

In the case of the Transformer, the size of the logits vector is equal to the number of words in the target dictionary. The raw prediction scores are normalized by the softmax function to generate a probability distribution. This distribution assigns to each entry in the dictionary the probability that it is the next output token. The entry with the highest probability is chosen as the output token for the current decoder time step.

An important observation is that the linear classification layer performs an operation that is the inverse of the token embedding operation at the decoder input. Recall that the token embedding operation projects a token from a known dictionary to a 512-dimensional embedding. The linear classifier projects a 512-dimensional embedding back to a dictionary of tokens. Therefore, certain optimized implementations use the values from the transposed version of the decoder's embedding matrix as the weights for this linear layer (since these are *always* inverse operations).

### *1.2.2.3. Decoder Stack Operation*

Figure 1.11 illustrates the operation of the Transformer decoder stack at a number of decoding time steps in our example of machine translation from English to French. The input sentence My favorite animal is the cat has been processed by the encoder stack to generate a set of embeddings. The embeddings have been projected onto two learnable 512-dimensional vector spaces to yield a matrix of values $\mathbf{V}_{enc}$ and a matrix of keys $\mathbf{K}_{enc}$. These vectors are consumed by every decoder in the stack, at every time step, to generate the target sentence in French.

At the first decoding time step, since no output tokens have been generated yet, the first decoder in the stack receives a special start-of-sequence (**[SOS]**) token embedding as input. The decoder processes this token to generate an embedding which is processed by the next decoder. The process continues until the last decoder in the stack generates the first target token, which, assuming a well-trained Transformer model, should map to the first target word Mon from the output (French) dictionary. This token is embedded and positionally encoded to generate the second embedding input to the decoder stack. The embeddings for the original **[SOS]** token and this new token are fed to the decoder stack in the next decoding time step. The decoder stack consumes these embeddings to produce two output tokens, the second of which should yield the next word animal in the target sentence. This word is used to generate the third input embedding which, together with the first two input embeddings, is fed to the decoder stack in the next time step and so on.

In figure 1.11, the underlined words at each time step indicate the new outputs that are generated by the decoder stack during that time step. As noted earlier, the output tokens from the previous

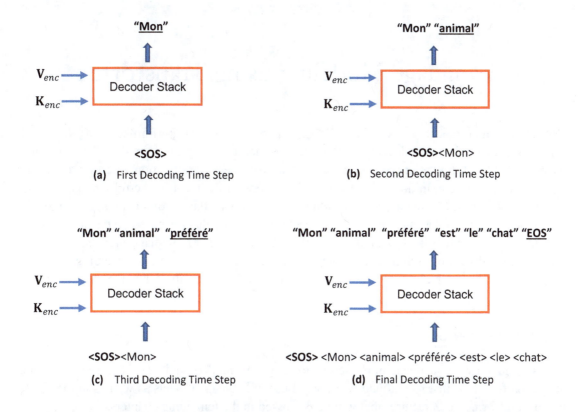

**Figure 1.11** Illustration of the Transformer Decoding Time Steps in the Machine Translation Example (<.> indicate input embeddings at the decoder, underlined embeddings indicate the newest outputs).

time steps need not be regenerated at every time step since the computations and outputs from the previous time steps can be stored and re-used to minimize the computational workload.

This process of output generation continues until the decoder stack has generated the target French sequence Mon animal préféré est le chat. Since the Transformer model has been trained to recognize that it has completed the translation task, it generates a special end-of-sequence (EOS) symbol at the next decoding time step. This ends the operations of the decoder stack until a new input sentence is processed by the encoder.

# 2. Language Modeling using Transformers

The Transformer model was originally designed to improve the performance of NLP tasks. Therefore, an obvious application of the Transformer architecture is in the development of language models for a variety of NLP tasks such as sentiment classification, question answering, textural entailment etc. In this chapter, we look at a few of the most impactful language models that are based on the Transformer architecture. There are two flavors of such language models - ones that are based on the encoder stack architecture and those that are based on the decoder stack architecture. We will look at examples of both of these classes of language models. Section 2.1 lays the groundwork of preliminary concepts that are essential tools in understanding the rest of this chapter. The remaining sections dive into the details of specific language models such as BERT and GPT.

## 2.1. Preliminaries

The section provides a quick introduction to language models and describes two non-linear activation functions that have found widespread use in language models as well as in the vision-based Transformer architectures that will be discussed in the remaining chapters.

### 2.1.1. Language Models

A language model is a concise representation of a large number of probability distributions over words or groups of words from a particular language. Practical language models are neural networks which analyze an input body of text to learn language patterns. The probability distributions that are learned during training are used to refine the values of the network weights. The learned distributions reflect the nature of the text database (or corpus) used during training. Given a new unseen context, which could consist of a single word or an incomplete sentence, a trained language model is able to generate the group of words that is most likely to follow.

Such a model could also be employed in other NLP tasks such as classifying the sentiment in a piece of text, summarizing a paragraph or declaring if an ordered pair of sentences (known as premise and hypothesis) are logically connected (textual entailment). This is done by fine-tuning a single pre-trained language model to each target task. Fine-tuning refers to the process of adjusting the weights of a pre-trained model while keeping the architecture unchanged. Language models vary in the underlying architecture of the neural network and in their complexity measured by the number of trainable parameters. In this chapter, we discuss the most popular language models that are based on the Transformer architecture. These language models use the self-attention mechanism in the Transformer architecture to build language contexts during the training process. For reasons that will soon become clear, the BERT model is built upon the Transformer encoder stack architecture, whereas GPT and its variant language models are based on the Transformer decoder stack architecture.

## 2.1.2. GELU and Hyperbolic Tangent

The RELU activation function, which is used exclusively in the original Transformer architecture, outputs a value of zero if the input parameter is negative and passes the input unchanged otherwise. It is therefore a function that is gated by the sign, rather than the value, of the input. The Gaussian error linear unit (GELU) function was introduced as an alternative network activation function that is gated by the value of the input variable instead of its sign. It has gained widespread use in neural networks because it results in better performance when compared to using the RELU. GELU is derived from the cumulative distribution function (CDF) of a Gaussian random variable $R$ with a mean of 0 and standard deviation of 1. The CDF of the random variable $R$ evaluated at a real-valued variable $y$ is the probability that $R \leq y$, and is computed as,

$$Pr(\{R \leq y\}) = \frac{1}{\sqrt{2\pi}} \int_{-\infty}^{y} e^{\frac{-t^2}{2}} dt$$

The output of the GELU function for a real-valued input variable $x$ is given by the product of $x$ and the probability that $R \leq x$.

$$GELU(x) = x.Pr(\{R \leq x\}) = \frac{x}{\sqrt{2\pi}} \int_{-\infty}^{x} e^{\frac{-t^2}{2}} dt$$

Since the integral above has no closed form solution, several approximations have been introduced over the years. One of the most recently proposed approximations [2] for the integral is commonly used in implementing the GELU function in practical neural network implementations. The closed-form GELU approximation is given by,

$$GELU(x) \approx 0.5x \left[ 1 + tanh\left( \sqrt{\frac{2}{\pi}} . \{x + 0.044715x^3\} \right) \right]; \quad tanh(a) = \frac{e^a - e^{-a}}{e^a + e^{-a}}$$

The RELU function and the approximated GELU function are plotted on the left in figure 2.1. The functions behave differently in the approximate input range of (-3.5, 3.5), and virtually overlap outside this range. While the RELU activation function always generates a non-negative output, the GELU can generate negative values.

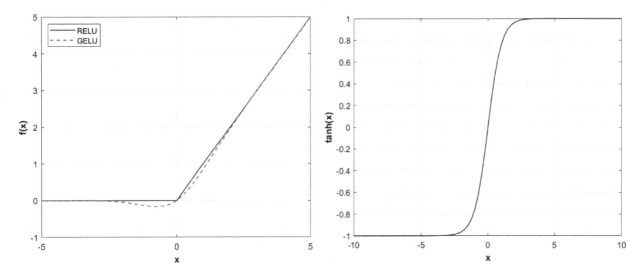

**Figure 2.1** Common Non-linear Activation Functions - (left) GELU, (right) hyperbolic tangent.

Moreover, the hyperbolic tangent (tanh) function itself is commonly employed as an activation function in feed-forward networks used for classification. As shown on the right in figure 2.1, the function is zero-centered and limits the output to a range of $(-1,1)$.

## 2.2. BERT

BERT was introduced in [3] and stands for *Bidirectional Encoder Representations from Transformers*. It is a *bidirectional* language model since it analyzes the tokens of the input sequence from left-to-right and right-to-left in order to build a language context. The model utilizes the self-attention mechanism in order to generate contexts between the input tokens. Due to its bidirectional nature, the BERT architecture is built upon the encoder stack in the Transformer model.

### 2.2.1. Model

The BERT model is a multi-layer stack of Transformer encoders based on the original implementation described in chapter 1. Two standard models (base and large), with different

| Model | Layers | Attention Heads | Embedding Size | #Parameters (Millions) |
|-------|--------|-----------------|----------------|------------------------|
| BERT-base | 12 | 12 | 768 | 110 |
| BERT-large | 24 | 16 | 1024 | 340 |

**Table 2.1** Configurations of the BERT Language Model.

complexities, were trained. Table 2.1 shows the architectural details of the two models. In both the models, the feed-forward layer in each encoder uses an expansion ratio of 4 and the GELU activation function for non-linearity.

## 2.2.2. WordPiece Tokenization

BERT was trained using the English language WordPiece embeddings with a vocabulary of 30,000 tokens. WordPiece is a tokenization approach based on generating tokens that represent pieces of words (sub-words), and not necessarily entire words, in the training text corpus. WordPiece starts with a small vocabulary that is made up of all of the characters in the training text. It breaks down words into sub-words, and initially these sub-words are generated by adding a prefix (##) to every character that is not the first character of a word. That is, each word is initially split by adding the prefix to all the characters inside the word (for example, the word **best** would be split into the sub-words b, ##e, ##s and ##t).

Thus, the initial alphabet in the vocabulary contains all the characters present at the beginning of a word and the characters present inside each word preceded by the WordPiece prefix. The algorithm then begins to merge pairs of these sub-words optimally using the frequencies of occurrence of the original sub-words and that of the merged sub-word. This is done by computing a score for each possible merged sub-word using the following equation.

$$score = \frac{frequency\ of\ merged\ subword}{(frequency\ of\ subword\ \#1)(frequency\ of\ subword\ \#2)}$$

The assigned score is the frequency of the merged sub-word divided by the product of the frequencies of each of its parts. At any point in the vocabulary building process, the pair of sub-words that yields the highest score is merged. The idea here is that a pair of sub-words is merged only if the frequency of the merged sub-word is higher than those of the contributing parts. It is easy to see that if this were not the case, the score computed for this pair would have a small value and this merging operation would have a low probability of going through. The merging process continues iteratively until a user-defined target size for the vocabulary is reached (30,000 tokens in the case of BERT).

An embedding table is used to map the final tokens to embeddings. The embedding table consists of as many rows as the number of entries in the vocabulary. Each entry in the vocabulary is assigned an independent value that is randomly initialized. These values are updated and learned along with the parameters of the language model during pre-training. This results in the generation of context-dependent embeddings for the tokens in the vocabulary.

The advantage of generating a vocabulary of sub-word tokens is that when an unfamiliar word is encountered during inference, an embedding can still be generated for the new word using the embeddings of its sub-words. As an example, assume that the training data consists of the prefix un (from words such as **unsure**, **unclear** etc.) and the words **characteristic** and **ally**, and that they are stored as three separate entries in the final vocabulary. Assume also that the word **uncharacteristically** was not present in the training corpus but is encountered during inference. This new word can be broken down into familiar component subwords as **uncharacteristically** = un + characteristic + ally. An embedding for the word **uncharacteristically** can now be generated by adding together the embeddings of the three subwords that are present in the pre-trained vocabulary. If a new word cannot be successfully processed in this manner, a special "unknown" token (**[UNK]**) is assigned to the word. The use of subwords minimizes the chances of employing the **[UNK]** tokens and therefore helps in boosting the performance of the language model.

### 2.2.3. Pre-training

The BERT model is pre-trained using two *unsupervised* methods, namely, *masked language modeling* (*MLM*) and *next sentence prediction* (*NSP*). MLM involves training the model using one contiguous sequence of tokens at a time (for tasks such as sentiment classification, tagging) and NSP uses two such sequences at a time (for tasks such as question-answering, textual entailment). These methods are discussed in detail in the following sections.

As the first step in pre-training, the words (tokens) in the input sequence(s) are mapped to their respective embeddings using the embedding table. A special learnable *classification token* (**[CLS]**) is always prepended to the input, and its purpose is to incrementally capture global information about the input data via the attention mechanism through the Transformer encoder layers. The corresponding embedding gathers data about the global characteristics of the input sequence(s) from each of the input embeddings during the successive attention computation operations. The output embedding corresponding to the **[CLS]** token is therefore used in classification tasks (entailment, sentiment classification). This output embedding is fed to a trained linear layer to generate the logit values over the target classes. This logit vector is then passed through a softmax layer to generate the probability distribution over the classes.

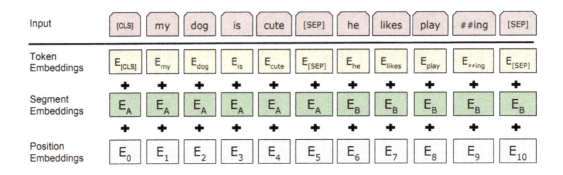

**Figure 2.2** Components of an Input Embedding (from [3]).

The end of a sequence in the input is indicated by a special delimiter token ([**SEP**]). In cases where the input consists of two sequences, a second [**SEP**] token is inserted between the two sequences. Additionally, when two sequences are fed to the model, a learned *segment embedding* is added to every token to indicate whether it belongs to the first or the second sequence. Finally, a learned position embedding is added to every input token in both the use cases. As shown in figure 2.2, the final input embedding for each token is the sum of the three embeddings. Two English language datasets were used in pre-training BERT – *BooksCorpus* with 800 million words and *English Wikipedia* with 2.5 billion words. The maximum length of the training input was set to 512 tokens. Note that the embeddings for all the special tokens that are used in pre-training, such as [**CLS**], [**SEP**] and [**MASK**] are also present in the embedding table.

### 2.2.3.1. Masked Language Modeling

The aim of MLM is to train the model to predict words in the input sentence that have been intentionally removed. A strictly left-to-right or right-to-left language model could be trained for this task by simply teaching it to predict the next word in the input sentence given the first few

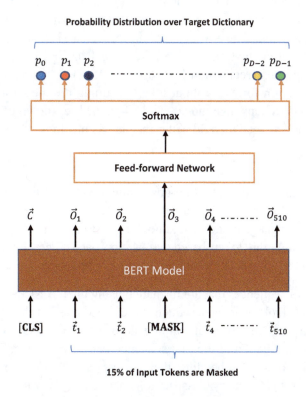

**Figure 2.3** Masked Language Modeling.

words. However, since BERT is a bidirectional model, this method of training would fail since the model is able to look at the entire input sequence in both directions and could simply learn to copy over the missing word.

The mechanism of MLM, illustrated in figure 2.3, is instead used to train the BERT language model. In this approach, 15% of the word locations in each input sequence are randomly chosen, and the corresponding tokens are replaced by a special **[MASK]** token. The model is trained to only predict the missing tokens rather than the entire input sequence. The output embedding that corresponds to each of the masked tokens is then passed through a feed-forward network (that inverts the tokenization process at the input) and then a softmax layer to generate a probability distribution over the input vocabulary. The most probable word based on this distribution is then assigned to the token. This process is repeated for each of the masked tokens in the input sequence. The language model and the feed-forward network are trained together using the cross-entropy loss function.

The actual implementation of the masking mechanism considers the fact that the **[MASK]** token is not encountered during fine-tuning or inference. Therefore, during pre-training, out of the 15% of the token locations that are selected for masking, the tokens are actually replaced by the **[MASK]** token 80% of the time, by a random token 10% of the time, and retained with no change the remaining 10% of the time. The advantage of this procedure is that it prevents the model from learning the bi-directional context only when it sees the **[MASK]** token in the input sequence. Since the original token is also retained in 1.5% (10% of 15%) of the cases, the model is forced to learn contextual information for every input token. Training the model in this manner helps in building a powerful generic language model. The 80-10-10 breakdown of token assignment was chosen in [3] because it was seen to yield better results when compared to other schemes.

### 2.2.3.2. Next Sentence Prediction

Many downstream language tasks (question-answering, textual entailment) require the model to understand the relationship between two sequences (each of which could contain multiple sentences of text). The language model would not be able to learn to derive such information if it were trained solely using the token-based MLM approach. Therefore, the BERT model is additionally trained to learn the relationship between pairs of sequences using the NSP method.

The model is fed pairs of sequences that are formatted using the **[CLS]** and **[SEP]** tokens as shown in figure 2.4. A few word tokens in each sequence are masked as per the MLM rules discussed in section 2.2.3.1. The aim of this type of training is to train the model to decide if the second sequence is a logical continuation of the first sequence in a piece of text. The classification label is generated using the output embedding that corresponds to the input **[CLS]** token. This embedding is passed through a binary classifier to generate an *isNext/notNext* classification label.

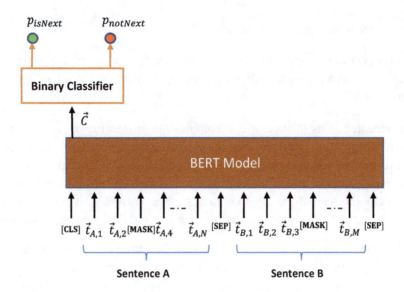

**Figure 2.4** Next Sentence Prediction.

The model and the classifier are again trained together. During pre-training, 50% of the training instances have sequences that actually follow each other in the training corpus, and the remaining 50% of the instances contain a randomly selected second sequence following the first sequence.

## 2.2.4. Fine-tuning

The pre-trained BERT language model, trained using the two methods discussed above, was fine-tuned for 11 NLP tasks in [3]. Fine-tuning involves the updating of all the parameters of the model using training examples that are specific to each target task.

Fine-tuning the BERT model for classification tasks such as text entailment and sentiment classification follow the process used in NSP pre-training. The fine-tuning process for other tasks (such as question-answering) differs significantly from the training process. In the question-answering task, the first sequence is the question to be answered, and the second sequence is the paragraph of text from which the answer to the question is to be determined. The BERT model generates two output sequences with the same lengths as the corresponding inputs. In fine-tuning for this task, two additional independent vectors (or linear layers) are trained - one for the start position of the answer in the second output sequence ($\vec{S}$), and the other for the end position of the answer ($\vec{E}$). These vectors have the same size as the output embeddings. An array of logit values is generated by computing the dot-product of the start vector with each of the output embeddings in the second sequence. This array is then passed through a softmax layer to generate a distribution that assigns a probability value to each token position of being the start index of the correct answer.

Mathematically, this computation can be denoted as $p_S(i) = \frac{e^{\vec{S}.\vec{O}_i}}{\sum_j e^{\vec{S}.\vec{O}_j}}$, where $\vec{O}_i$ is the $i^{th}$ output embedding, and $p_S(i)$ is the probability that $i$ is the starting index of the answer in the second input sequence. The token location with the highest probability is picked as the starting location for the correct answer.

This process is repeated using the vector $\vec{E}$ to compute the probability of each token position being the end location of the correct answer. During fine-tuning, the model as well as the start and end linear layers are trained together using the ground-truth data of a text corpus. An additional condition is imposed to ensure that the end location always occurs after the start location. The training objective is the sum of the log-likelihoods of the correct start and end positions, that is, the negative of the sum of the maximum start probability and the maximum end probability.

In the sentence completion task, given a sentence, the task is to choose the most plausible continuation among multiple choices. During fine-tuning, separate pairs of input sequences are created with each pair containing the given sentence followed by one of the choices for the possible continuation. The task-specific parameters in this case are the weights of a single vector (linear layer) whose dot-product with the **[CLS]** token's output embedding computes a score for each choice. The set of scores is normalized using a softmax layer to generate a probability value for each of the options. The option with the highest probability is chosen as the predicted output. The model and the linear layer are fine-tuned together using the ground-truth data from the training corpus.

It was seen that the BERT-large model performed consistently better than the BERT-base model over all the tasks. This is expected since a larger model is able to extract and learn more complex patterns in the training data when compared to a smaller model.

## 2.3. GPT

The *Generative Pre-trained Transformer* (GPT) is a language model that was introduced in [4] around the same time as the BERT model was. Generative pre-training refers to the approach of training a language model on a generic text corpus, and then fine-tuning it using task-specific datasets. This is similar to the approach that was used with the BERT model. The major differences between the two models are seen in their architectures - while BERT is a bidirectional model that is built upon the Transformer encoder stack, GPT is a unidirectional model that uses the Transformer decoder stack at its core. This is because GPT is auto-regressive in nature, which means that it generates the current output token based on the context of the previously generated tokens. The current output then becomes a part of the input context for the generation of the next output token, and so on. This property aligns with how the decoder stack in the Transformer architecture operates. Therefore, the GPT model and its variants are built upon the Transformer decoder stack with modifications to account for the absence of the inputs from the encoder stack.

## 2.3.1. Model

The language model, shown in figure 2.5, is a modified version of Transformer's decoder stack, and directly consumes the tokens generated from the input text. The GPT model consists of a stack of 12 modified Transformer decoders, each of which is missing the cross-attention blocks from figure 1.2. Each decoder consists of 12 masked self-attention heads that operate on embeddings of size 1×768. For the position-wise feed-forward networks, the hidden dimension is 1×3072 (4× expansion), and Gaussian Error Linear Unit (GELU) is used as the non-linear activation function. This model uses learnable position embeddings instead of the sinusoidal version used with the original Transformer. The model contains about 115 million learnable parameters.

The model is trained on a large unlabeled corpus of text data that is not specific to any task (hence the name generative pre-training). This is followed by fine-tuning, using datasets with task-specific annotations, which modifies the parameters of the model but leaves the architecture untouched.

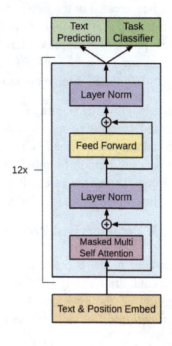

**Figure 2.5** Architecture of the GPT Language Model (from [4]).

## 2.3.2. Byte-pair Encoding Tokenization

GPT uses the *byte-pair encoding* (BPE) algorithm to generate the input tokens. BPE was introduced as a compression algorithm [5] but has found application in text tokenization. The training text corpus is normalized, which in the NLP realm, refers to reducing the variability of the data. Some of the processes involved in text normalization include conversion to lower-case letters, expansion of word contractions (we'll, haven't etc.) and stemming (retaining the base form of a word by eliminating suffixes and prefixes). A special delimiter is then appended to the end of every word in the normalized text, and the modified corpus is partitioned into individual characters and symbols (referred to collectively as characters in the rest of this discussion). This set of unique characters forms the base vocabulary that is fed to the BPE algorithm.

The BPE algorithm begins by counting the frequency of each character in the training corpus. In the first iteration, the algorithm merges the two most frequently occurring characters into a string. The newly created string is added to the base vocabulary and its frequency of occurrence is computed. It is possible that after the merging operation, one of the original characters no longer exists in the text corpus. In that case, the character is removed from the vocabulary. In the second iteration, the merging algorithm is applied to the entries in the updated vocabulary. This could result in the merging of two different characters or the addition of a new character to the string that was created in the first iteration. In either case, the newly created string is again added to the vocabulary. Entries that no longer exist in an unmerged form are removed from the vocabulary. This process is applied iteratively to the training corpus until the vocabulary reaches a predetermined size. The GPT model uses a base vocabulary of 478 characters and stops training after 40,000 BPE merge operations. Therefore, the final vocabulary has a size of 40,478 tokens.

Each token in the training sequence is converted to a 768-bit embedding by projecting it using a learned embedding matrix. Additionally, a learnable position embedding is added to the token embedding before it is fed to the Transformer decoder stack. The embedding matrix and position vectors are randomly initialized and are refined jointly with the model parameters during pre-training. As was the case with BERT, the language model is pre-trained in an unsupervised manner and fine-tuned using labelled task-specific data.

### 2.3.3. Unsupervised Pre-training

The GPT model is pre-trained on a sequence of tokens that are generated from a large corpus of text data. Pre-training of the language model involves the prediction of the current token given the context of the previous $k$ tokens. This ensures that the training can be performed in an unsupervised fashion, without the need for labeled data.

Consider a sequence of $n$ input tokens $\mathbf{T} = \{\vec{t}_1, \dots, \vec{t}_n\}$. The language model is trained to maximize the likelihood function expressed as $L_{pre-train} = \sum_i Pr(\vec{t}_i | \vec{t}_{i-1}, \vec{t}_{i-2}, \dots, \vec{t}_{i-k}; \Theta)$. Here, $k$ is the length of the context window and $Pr(. | .)$ indicates the conditional probability that is modeled using a set of parameters $\Theta$. In this case, the model parameters $\Theta$ correspond to a multi-layer stack of Transformer decoders.

In the steady operational state, one new input token is fed to the Transformer decoder stack, which generates one new output token. The sequence of operations of the Transformer decoder stack follows the description in section 1.2.2.2.3, with the exception of the cross-attention computation. Each token is converted to an embedding and positionally encoded using learnable parameters. The decoder stack produces one new output token, which is multiplied by the transpose of the learnable embedding matrix to generate a vector of logits whose size is equal to the number of entries in the input dictionary. The logits vector is passed through a softmax function to generate the probability distribution over all the target tokens. The training process aims to maximize the likelihood function $L_{pre-train}$ at each step.

The GPT language model was pre-trained in [4] using the *BooksCorpus* dataset that contains long stretches of contiguous text from nearly 7000 unique unpublished books across genres. Since a context window size of $k = 512$ tokens was used, an array of 512 position embeddings was randomly initialized and learned during pre-training.

## 2.3.4. Supervised Fine-tuning

The pre-trained language model is fine-tuned for a target task using labeled data that is specific to the task. For a text classification task, the labeled dataset that is used to fine-tune the model is made up of classification instances, where each instance consists of a sequence of input tokens, $\mathbf{X} = \{\vec{x}_1, \dots, \vec{x}_m\}$ and a corresponding classification label $y$. The fine-tuning process involves passing the tokens in each training instance ($\mathbf{X}$) through the pre-trained model to obtain a sequence of output embeddings $\{\vec{h}_1, \dots, \vec{h}_m\}$ from the last decoder in the stack. The output embedding $\vec{h}_m$, which corresponds to the last input token $\vec{x}_m$, is then fed into a linear layer. This embedding is chosen because it is the only embedding that is generated by the GPT model using the context of the entire input sequence. In other words, the last output token for a given input sequence is considered to be a *representation* of the entire sequence. The vector output from the linear layer is passed through a softmax layer to generate a probability distribution over the target classes. This distribution can be denoted mathematically as $Pr(y|\vec{x}_1, \dots, \vec{x}_m)$ since it represents the likelihood of predicting the classification label $y$ given the sequence of input tokens $\mathbf{X}$. The fine-tuning objective, which is to maximize this likelihood function over all of the training instances, can be expressed as $L_{fine-tune} = \sum_{(\mathbf{X},y)} Pr(y|\mathbf{X})$.

It was found that better model generalization and faster training could be achieved if the likelihood functions from both the pre-training and fine-tuning stages were combined into a single fine-tuning objective. That is, the objective function to be optimized during fine-tuning is given by $L_{final} = L_{pre-train} + \lambda L_{fine-tune}$, where $\lambda$ is the Lagrange multiplier that controls the relative importance of the two terms.

Other NLP tasks use structured inputs that consist of more than one sequence of tokens. Since the pre-trained model was trained on contiguous sequences of text, additional learnable tokens are added to introduce a sense of order into the input data when the model is fine-tuned for such tasks. Figure 2.6 shows the three types of tokens that are used across a variety of tasks - **[start]** and **[extract]** respectively indicate the beginning and end of a training instance, whereas the **[delimiter]** token indicates that the training instance consists of multiple related sequences. The usage of these non-text tokens is significant because it circumvents the need to modify the model architecture based on the specific data formats for each task. The embeddings for these tokens are randomly initialized and are learned during the fine-tuning process.

The task of textual entailment uses an ordered pair of input sentences, where the premise is followed by the hypothesis. The function of the language model is to then determine whether the hypothesis follows from the premise. This is a specific application of a generic classification task, where the output embedding corresponding to the last input token is passed through a binary classifier to generate a prediction.

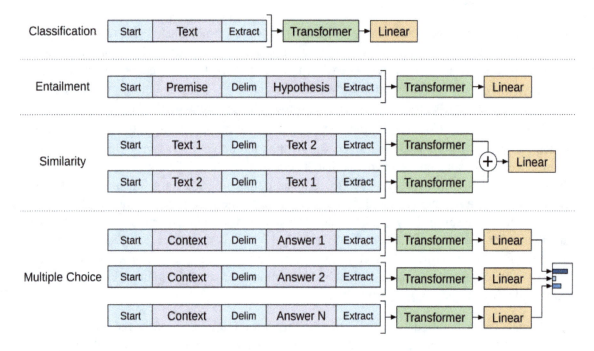

**Figure 2.6** Structure of the Input Data for Various NLP Tasks (from [4]).

As shown in figure 2.6, the task of estimating the similarity between two sentences could encounter the sentences in any order. The fine-tuning process for this task generates two input sequences to account for the two possible sentence orderings (with a delimiter in between the two sentences). Each input sequence is processed independently to produce an output sequence of embeddings. The last output embedding from each of the runs is picked, and the two embeddings are added element-wise to generate a composite output embedding. This embedding is passed through a binary classifier to generate a prediction.

In the case of question answering with multiple choices for the answer, each training instance consists of a document, a question and a set of answer choices. The document and the question are concatenated into a single context sequence and attached to each possible answer, along with a delimiter token in between. This yields as many input sequences per training instance as there are answers, and each of these sequences is processed independently by the pre-trained model. The last output embedding for each sequence is then passed through a linear layer, and the results are passed through a softmax layer that generates an output probability distribution over the possible answers.

## 2.4. GPT-2

The GPT-2 language model [6] introduced the concept of multitask learning in which the model is pre-trained but is not fine-tuned for specific NLP tasks. In this approach, a large-capacity language model is pre-trained in an unsupervised manner on a large and diverse text corpus so that it begins to learn generalizations about the language as a whole. It was shown that a language model that is trained in this manner acquires the ability to excel at a range of NLP tasks without having to be fine-tuned explicitly with task-specific data. This approach is significant because it eliminates the burden of having to generate large amounts of labeled data for each target task. The keys to the success of multitask learning are a high-complexity language model and an enormous amount of diverse generic training text data.

In [6], the text corpus for pre-training was generated by scraping the web for pages that have been curated and/or rated by humans. The resulting dataset, known as *WebText*, contains the filtered text of nearly 45 million web links. Textual content was extracted from these links and cleaned up with some heuristic-based post-processing. The final training corpus consisted of over 8 million documents for a total of 40 GB of text. This is diverse enough to serve as a general corpus for language modeling.

The GPT-2 model is based on the GPT architecture, but with a few modifications. Referring to figure 2.5, in the GPT-2 architecture, layer normalization is applied to the signal prior to the self-attention layer and an additional layer normalization operation is applied to the signal after the final self-attention layer in the stack. Just like in the GPT architecture, each decoder layer consists of 12 masked self-attention heads.

GPT-2 improved upon the BPE tokenization scheme by applying the algorithm at the byte level instead of the character level as was done in GPT. As discussed in section 2.3.2, the BPE algorithm begins with a base vocabulary of characters which is augmented with new entries that are generated by a large number of a frequency-based merging operation. The problem with the character-based approach is that it cannot produce a vocabulary of manageable size that can be used to represent any possible input word using some combination of subwords in the vocabulary. But this is an essential requirement for a powerful generic language model that can perform a variety of tasks without any fine-tuning. Therefore, GPT-2 operates on individual bytes in the character representations and begins with a base vocabulary of all the 256 possible byte values and a special end-of-text token. The byte merging operations are performed as per the rule described for the BPE algorithm in section 2.3.2. The final GPT-2 vocabulary had a size of 50,257 tokens. GPT-2 is similar to GPT in using a learned embedding matrix to map these tokens to embeddings.

GPT-2 is pre-trained using the same objective function and procedure as those that are used to train the GPT model. Given the context of a set of input tokens, the aim is to predict the next token in the sequence. GPT-2 uses an input context window size of 1024 tokens.

Four language models, with increasing complexity (or capacity), were trained using the procedure discussed above. The architectural details of these models are listed in table 2.2. The smallest model is equivalent to the original GPT model, and the second smallest model is equivalent to the BERT-large

| Layers ($L$) | Hidden Size ($D$) | #Parameters (Millions) |
|---|---|---|
| 12 | 768 | 117 |
| 24 | 1024 | 345 |
| 36 | 1280 | 762 |
| 48 | 1600 | 1542 (GPT-2) |

**Table 2.2**  Variants of the GPT-2 Language Model.

model (table 2.1). The largest model is known as the official GPT-2 model and consists of 1.5 billion trainable parameters, which is nearly ten times the number of parameters in the GPT model.

According to [6], the GPT-2 model was tested on eight target language tasks. Before each test, the language model was conditioned to the specifics about each target task. This was accomplished via textual interactions with the model using a few example data instances. Each data instance consisted of an input sequence, an optional title of the task and an output sequence which was the expected output.

For example, the model was conditioned for a language translation task (say, English to French) by feeding it a series of examples in the format: English sentence = "abc", French sentence = "xyz", English sentence = "def", French sentence = "uvw", and so on. Then, when the model was prompted with just English sentence = "fgh", it was able to lean upon its general pre-training and learn from the example instances to complete the task by generating the translated French sentence. Likewise, a reading comprehension training example to condition the model could be formatted as (answer the question, document, question, answer).

This method of conditioning the pre-trained model using examples and a prompt was used for all of the target tasks over which GPT-2 was evaluated. It was seen that the model was able to learn what it was supposed to do just through these interactions and without any form of fine-tuning. As expected, the complexity of the language model was seen to be indicative of the performance of the model on the tasks. Results showed that the performance of the four models listed in table 2.2 improved in a log-linear fashion, across tasks, with increasing complexity.

In seven of the eight cases, the largest GPT-2 model was able to meet or beat the performance of models that were specially trained for the respective tasks. This shows the power of training a high-capacity language model on a large generic text dataset such as *WebText*.

## 2.5. GPT-3

GPT-3 extends the concept of a pre-trained model that can learn to perform a variety of tasks using prompts and demonstrations without requiring any fine-tuning [7]. The motivation was to develop a language model that would mimic the human ability to learn to perform a new language task from a few examples or from simple instructions.

This led to the development of the concept of *meta-learning* or *in-context learning* and resulted in the GPT-3 language model. In meta-learning, the language model is pre-trained in a large data corpus but is not fine-tuned for any of the target tasks. Instead, a simple description or title of the task is fed to the pretrained language model and is followed by pairs of examples of input sequences and the corresponding output sequence. The model is then fed an incomplete example or a *prompt*, which consists of just the input sequence, and the language model is expected to have learned to "complete the sentence" by generating the correct output sequence based on the task at hand.

The leap in the performance of the GPT-3 model compared to the earlier versions of GPT is fueled by two major factors – the complexity/capacity of the model (175 billion parameters), and the gigantic size of the pre-training text corpus (45 TB).

| Model | Layers ($L$) | Attention Heads ($A$) | Hidden Size ($D$) | #Parameters (Millions) |
|---|---|---|---|---|
| GPT-3 Small | 12 | 12 | 768 | 125 |
| GPT-3 Medium | 24 | 16 | 1024 | 350 |
| GPT-3 Large | 24 | 16 | 1536 | 760 |
| GPT-3 XL | 24 | 24 | 2048 | 1300 |
| GPT-3 2.7B | 32 | 32 | 3560 | 2700 |
| GPT-3 6.7B | 32 | 32 | 4096 | 6700 |
| GPT-3 13B | 40 | 40 | 5140 | 13000 |
| "GPT-3" | 96 | 96 | 12288 | 175000 |

**Table 2.3** Variants of the GPT-3 Language Model.

## 2.5.1. Model

GPT-3 is just a vastly scaled-up version of the base architecture of GPT-2. The only modification is the replacement of every second Transformer decoder block with one that uses a lower-complexity factorized approximation of the attention computation [8]. Several flavors with increasing capacity, ranging from 125 million parameters to 175 billion parameters, were trained (shown in table 2.3), with the largest model known as GPT-3. This language model consists of 96 Transformer decoder layers (without the cross-attention layers). Each decoder layer consists of

128 masked attention heads and uses embeddings of size 1x12228 (with an expansion factor of 4 in the feed-forward network).

## 2.5.2. Pre-training

The GPT-3 language model was pre-trained using a large text corpus that is made up of a few different datasets. Table 2.4 shows the contributing sources and the composition of the text corpus. *Common Crawl* is a publicly available web archive that contains text that has been extracted from the internet after the removal of markup and other non-text content. This process produces around 20TB of scraped

| Dataset | Total Tokens | Weight in Training Mix |
|---|---|---|
| Filtered Common Crawl | 410 billion | 60% |
| WebText2 | 19 billion | 22% |
| Books1 | 12 billion | 8% |
| Books2 | 55 billion | 8% |
| Wikipedia | 3 billion | 3% |

**Table 2.4**  Composition of GPT-2 Training Data.

text data each month but consists of a wide variety of non-natural language text such as source code, menu lists, inappropriate and nonsensical text and duplicated data. This dataset is heavily filtered to generate usable natural language text data that makes up the majority of the pre-training text corpus. *WebText2* is an enhanced dataset version of *WebText* that was used in GPT-2 pre-training. *Books1* (also known as *BookCorpus*) is a large collection of free novels written by unpublished authors and contains the text of 11,038 books. Details about *Books2* are not publicly available.

The term "Weight in training mix" in table 2.4 refers to the fraction of examples that are drawn from the corresponding datasets during training. The text in these datasets was converted into tokens using the byte-level BPE algorithm that was also used for GPT-2. The final training data for GPT-3 consisted of a total of 300 billion tokens. The size of the input context window was increased to 2048 tokens.

## 2.5.3. Performance

The GPT-3 model proved that scaling up language models and the size of the training corpus could indeed enable models to perform favorably in a few-shot environment in comparison to specialized fine-tuned state-of-the-art models. The pre-trained GPT-3 model was applied to a variety of natural language tasks without any fine-tuning, with the task and few-shot demonstrations specified purely via text interaction with the model. Figure 2.7 illustrates the differences between the traditional fine-tuning approach used with models such as BERT and GPT, and the zero-shot, one-shot and few-shot interactions used with GPT-3.

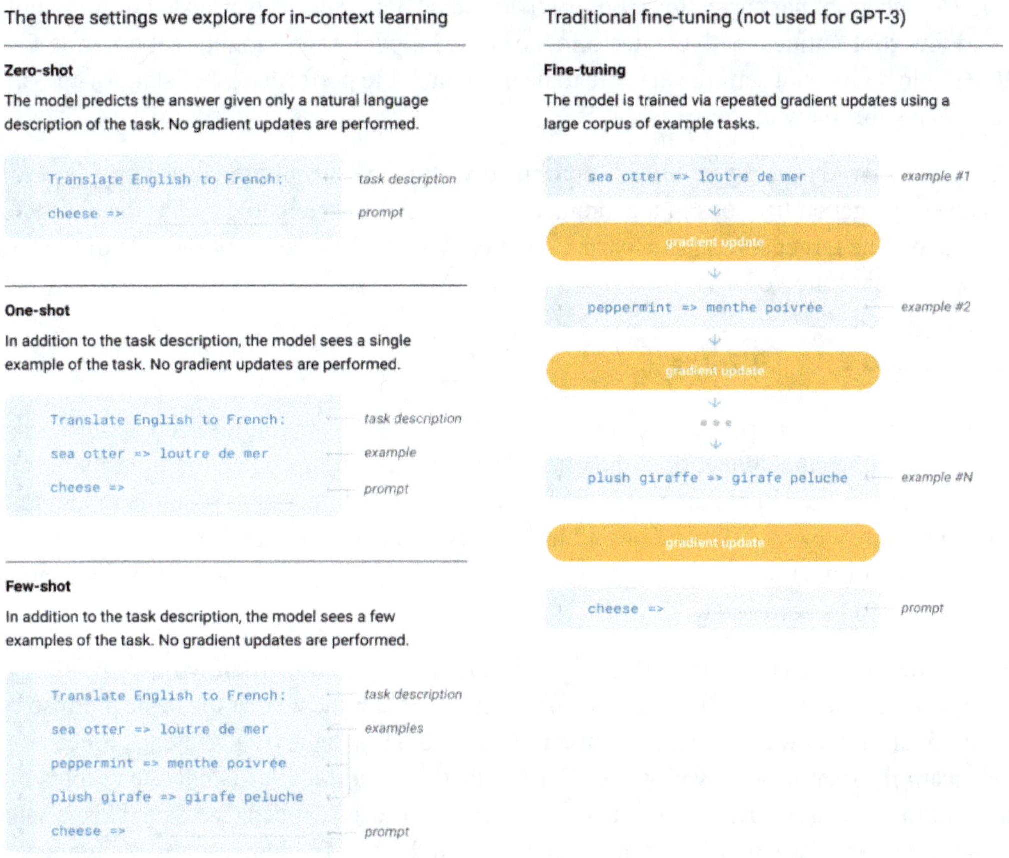

The three settings we explore for in-context learning

Traditional fine-tuning (not used for GPT-3)

**Zero-shot**

The model predicts the answer given only a natural language description of the task. No gradient updates are performed.

```
Translate English to French:     ← task description
cheese =>                        ← prompt
```

**Fine-tuning**

The model is trained via repeated gradient updates using a large corpus of example tasks.

```
sea otter => loutre de mer       ← example #1
             ↓
        gradient update
             ↓
peppermint => menthe poivrée     ← example #2
             ↓
        gradient update
             ↓
            • • •
             ↓
plush giraffe => girafe peluche  ← example #N
             ↓
        gradient update
```

**One-shot**

In addition to the task description, the model sees a single example of the task. No gradient updates are performed.

```
Translate English to French:     ← task description
sea otter => loutre de mer       ← example
cheese =>                        ← prompt
```

**Few-shot**

In addition to the task description, the model sees a few examples of the task. No gradient updates are performed.

```
Translate English to French:     ← task description
sea otter => loutre de mer       ← examples
peppermint => menthe poivrée
plush girafe => girafe peluche
cheese =>                        ← prompt
```

```
cheese =>                        ← prompt
```

**Figure 2.7** Language Model Fine-tuning (BERT, GPT) versus In-context Learning (GPT-3) (from [7]).

For each task, GPT-3 was evaluated under 3 conditions:

- "few-shot learning", or in-context learning where several demonstrations of the task were allowed. The number of demonstrations was limited by the number of tokens in the context window,
- "one-shot learning," where a single demonstration of the task was allowed, and
- "zero-shot" learning, where no demonstrations were allowed and only a natural language instruction was given to the model.

GPT-3 achieved strong performance on many traditional NLP tasks (sentence completion, question answering, translation), and others that require on-the-fly reasoning or domain adaptation (common-sense reasoning, reading comprehension, arithmetic operations of addition, subtraction (2-, 3-, 4- and 5-digit numbers) and 2-digit multiplication, unscrambling words, news article completion and grammar correction). For each task, the GPT-3 model was tested in zero-shot, one-shot and few-shot settings, with the performance of the model improving in that order. It was seen that GPT-3 in a few-shot setting was able to nearly match the performance of state-of-the-art fine-tuned systems for many of these tasks.

The extremely large capacity of GPT-3 combined with the vast training corpus enable it to learn the nuances and generalizations in the language. The model was able to develop the ability to pick up clues about the target task and to learn dynamically from the context of the title of the task and example data that followed.

## 2.6. GPT-3.5 and ChatGPT

*ChatGPT* is an extremely popular commercial platform that has revolutionized applications such as online search, document creation and question answering. It has gained popularity because its responses nearly mimic how humans interact with one other. Interaction with the model involves the use of prompts and questions from a human user in a *zero-shot* setting. That is, the user can ask a question or direct the model to generate a document without having to provide examples of how the task is to be performed.

These abilities are made possible by the underlying language model known as GPT-3.5, which was originally introduced in [9] as *InstructGPT*. The authors indicate that the basic premise behind developing this model was to *align* the outputs of the model with the user's intents. Since language models learn from large-scale web-scraped datasets, they could learn to generate outputs that are untruthful, toxic, biased or in some manner not what the user expected to see. This is what the authors refer to as a lack of alignment between the model and the human user. Alignment could be explicit (for example, following instructions provided by the user) or implicit (for example, not making up facts). The method that was used in [9] to help achieve alignment is known as *reinforcement learning from human feedback* (RLHF). It uses human preferences as a reward signal to adjust the model's behavior, which is important because safety and alignment issues are often complex and subjective and cannot be fully captured using automated objective metrics.

At the core of the GPT-3.5 language model is a pre-trained GPT-3 model. The lack of alignment of the GPT-3 model arises because all that it is trained to do is predict the next word based on the specific input context. It is not trained to generate an output based on a human user's expectations. GPT-3.5 is a GPT-3 language model that has been intentionally fine-tuned (using supervised learning and reinforcement learning) to produce results that align with the intents of human users. This process, which consists of three stages, uses the large database of prompts that have been submitted to the OpenAI API which is public user interface to the core language model.

In the first stage, a team of people was hired to manually generate responses to a sampling of these prompts which cover a wide variety of language tasks. The pre-trained GPT-3 model was then fine-tuned in a supervised fashion using the human-generated responses to various types of language prompts. In the second stage, a different sampling of the OpenAI API prompts was fed to a set of language models in order to generate several responses to each of the prompts. A team of trained human labelers manually assigned ratings, to the responses of each prompt, to indicate their order of preference. This data was used to train a reward model which predicts human-preferred output. In the final stage, this reward model was then used to further refine the language model iteratively using reinforcement learning. The resulting model is known as GPT-3.5 (originally *InstructGPT*) and is the basis of the *ChatGPT* application.

GPT-3.5 was tested with public datasets that are designed to capture aspects of language model safety, such as truthfulness, toxicity and bias. It showed improvements in alignment and truthfulness, and reductions in toxic output generation, while having minimal performance regressions on academic NLP datasets. The results from a GPT-3.5 model based on the 1.3 billion parameter GPT-3 XL model (see table 2.3) were preferred by human labelers to those from the *original* 175 billion parameter GPT-3 model. Note that the original GPT-3 model consists of 130x the number of parameters. Additionally, the model also performed consistently on other NLP datasets that measure zero-shot performance on standard NLP tasks such as question answering, reading comprehension, and summarization. The model has shown good performance on non-traditional NLP tasks such as source code generation and code summarization.

# 3. The Vision Transformer

The Transformer model resulted from the need to improve the performance of NLP tasks and has found widespread application in that field. On the other hand, tasks in the field of computer vision have until recently employed pure convolutional neural networks or hybrid ones where a few convolutional layers are replaced by self-attention layers. Although CNNs excel at extracting local features, they lack the ability to capture global correlations between the different parts of an image. This is a disadvantage when CNNs are used for high-level computer vision tasks since these tasks generally benefit from the availability of such global information. The Vision Transformer (ViT) [10] aims to solve this problem through the application of the self-attention mechanism to image data.

The ViT targets the vision task of image classification using just the encoder half of the original Transformer architecture. This task was chosen because it is a core application in computer vision and is often used as a benchmark to measure the progress that has been made in general image understanding. Improved performance in this task usually translates to improvements in other related tasks such as object detection and scene segmentation. When trained on large datasets (14M-300M images), the ViT was able to achieve better performance than the state-of-the-art CNNs (residual networks). However, when the Vision Transformer was trained on mid-sized datasets (1M – 10M images), its performance was slightly inferior in comparison to residual networks of a similar size. The performance of the ViT was therefore achieved at the cost of having to use extensive resources to train it on very large databases.

Convolutional networks use filters with limited regions of support and benefit from operating on strongly correlated pixels in local regions of an image. This property, that is often referred to as *inductive bias*, helps CNNs in generalizing their learning. However, CNNs lack the ability to extract global correlations across the different regions of an image. On the other hand, the ViT architecture uses the self-attention mechanism to extract image-level connections but suffers from the absence of inductive bias. The need for more extensive training in the case of the ViT was attributed to this shortcoming. Nevertheless, the ViT represents an important first step in extending the Transformer model architecture to the field of computer vision.

The ViT architecture is the encoder half of the original Transformer with a few modifications. It is made up of a stack of encoder layers, each of which has a structure that closely resembles the encoder layer of the original Transformer. The differences in data processing and architecture, which will be discussed in the following sections, arise because the ViT operates on images whereas the original Transformer worked with text data.

## 3.1. Preliminaries

This section introduces a few key terms that are used extensively in our discussions on the Vision Transformer and other related architectures. This discussion assumes a basic understanding of how images are processed by convolutional neural networks.

### 3.1.1. Pre-Normalization and Post-Normalization

In the Transformer architecture, layer normalization (see section 1.2.1.2.3) is used to reduce the variability of the data that is generated by the self-attention (SA) layers and the feed-forward networks (FFN). In the original Transformer architecture as well as in its early variations, layer normalization was applied to the signal that resulted from combining the output from a particular sub-layer (SA/FFN) with the input signal to that layer (through a skip connection). That is, layer normalization was a part of the post-processing operation of the signal from a layer. This implementation is therefore known as *post-normalization* and is illustrated in figure 3.1(a).

Post-normalization works well in the original Transformer architecture with a stack of six encoders. However, subsequent work [11] has shown that using post-normalization leads to gradient issues when training deeper Transformer architectures. The gradients either vanish or explode during training, and this leads to sub-optimal learning and inferior performance. Better results were obtained with these architectures when layer normalization was applied to the signal prior to the processing by the self-attention layer or FFN. The modified design is known as *pre-normalization* and is illustrated in figure 3.1(b). It should be noted that both of these methods were found to be good choices for a Transformer with six encoder layers. The benefit of using pre-normalization is pronounced in deeper models such as the ViT.

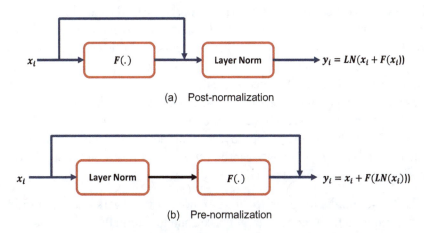

(a)  Post-normalization

(b)  Pre-normalization

**Figure 3.1** Approaches to Layer Normalization.

### 3.1.2. Multi-Layer Perceptron (MLP) and Classification Head

A *multi-layer perceptron* is a feed-forward neural network with one or more non-linear activation layers. Every encoder and decoder layer in the original Transformer architecture consists of a two-layer feed-forward network with a RELU activation layer in between. The corresponding network used in ViT encoders is known as an MLP and is similar in structure, except for the use of the GELU as the activation function.

When the ViT is used for image classification, a specially designated output token is fed to an MLP network known as a *classification head*. This network consists of two linear layers with a hyperbolic tangent activation function in between them. It is used to map the special output token of the ViT to prediction values over a known number of classes. The raw unnormalized predictions at the output of the classification head are then converted to a probability distribution using a softmax function. This distribution is used to generate a final class prediction.

### 3.1.3. Network Fine-tuning

Fine-tuning is the process of adapting a trained neural network to a task that is different from the one for which it was originally trained. It also refers to the situation where, at inference time, the network is fed with images whose characteristics vary significantly from the data that was used at training time. Fine-tuning is widely used to adapt standard CNNs such as residual networks for a range of computer vision tasks. Training a completely new CNN for every new vision task is expensive in terms of computational power, time and effort. Therefore, CNNs that have been pre-trained for a basic vision task are usually fine-tuned for related tasks. The original task and database are referred to as the source task and database respectively, and the new task and database are the target task and database.

Fine-tuning is possible because layers in the different parts of a CNN learn image filters that extract different kinds of features from the input image. It has been shown that the first few layers learn to detect basic high-level features such as edges and corners in the image, the next few layers usually learn to detect slightly more advanced features, and the last few layers normally learn filters that extract features that are very specific to the source task. The complexity of the learnable filters increases with the depth of the network. If such a CNN were retrained for a different vision task, the earlier layers would still learn to detect the same basic features such as edges and corners as they did for the first task, and the deeper layers would learn new sets of filters. Therefore, the filters from the earlier layers of the CNN can be reused for various target applications, whereas the deeper layers might need to be retrained.

The idea behind fine-tuning is to retain (or *freeze*) most of the layers that learn to identify basic features, which is required for a range of target tasks, and to retrain the last few layers that usually learn features that are very specific to the source database and the source task. During the fine-tuning process, the last few layers of the trained network are replaced by new randomly initialized layers. The sizes and number of these replacement layers are tailored to the specifics of the target task and database, and only the new layers are trained from scratch. The weights of the frozen (or pre-trained) layers are retained and only finely adjusted for optimal performance.

### 3.1.4. Visual Task Adaptation Benchmark (VTAB)

An important goal of machine vision research is to design networks that have the ability to learn general and useful features (or *visual representations*) that are task-agnostic. Specifically, the aim is to design a network that is pre-trained once on a large dataset but is able to perform well on a wide range of vision tasks without having to be retrained specifically for each task. This approach, known as *representation learning*, aims to eliminate the need to generate expensive labelled datasets for each specific task and to have to train networks from scratch for each new task. The networks that are pre-trained in this manner should perform well at each target task with just a small amount of task-specific fine-tuning. In order to measure progress towards this goal, researchers need a standard set of data and metrics to benchmark the performance of existing and new networks. This had led to the introduction of the *visual task adaptation benchmark* (VTAB) [12].

VTAB is an evaluation mechanism that is designed to measure the progress in developing networks that can learn general and useful visual representations. It consists of a suite of nineteen evaluation vision tasks for a test network to complete. These networks generally use their learned visual representations in order to perform these tasks, and must satisfy two specific requirements:

- They must not be pre-trained on any of the data (labels or input images) used in the downstream evaluation tasks, and,
- They must not contain hardcoded, task-specific logic, and must treat the evaluation tasks like previously unseen tasks.

These constraints are in place to ensure that networks that perform well on VTAB will be able to generalize to any future tasks. VTAB prohibits the pre-training of the test network on the evaluation tasks. Rather, the pre-trained test network must be adapted to solve new tasks with limited task-specific data.

The 19 representative vision tasks (and the respective datasets), over which a test network is to be evaluated, are categorized into 3 classes:

- **Natural**: classical vision tasks to be performed on natural images that have been captured using regular cameras.
- **Specialized**: same tasks as in the Natural class but performed on images that have been captured using special equipment. The two main classes in this group are remote-sensing and medical imaging.

- **Structured**: tasks that test the scene perception ability of the test network, like object counting, orientation detection and depth perception.

While highly diverse, all of the tasks in VTAB share one common feature which is that humans can complete them relatively easily after training on just a few examples. A test model could be pre-trained for a related but different vision task and needs to be adapted to the specific VTAB tasks. The simplest adaptation strategy in deep representation learning is to first pre-train the network, then freeze the network's weights and train another, usually smaller, model to operate on the outputs of the pre-trained model. Alternatively, when the upstream and downstream datasets differ significantly, fine-tuning the original weights has been found to be more effective. Note that VTAB does not constrain the strategy used to adapt the test model for any of the tasks.

In the *VTAB-1k* database, 1000 labelled examples (800 for training and 200 for validation) are provided for each task on which the model is tested. A larger database known as *VTAB-full* consists of a larger number of examples for each task.

## 3.2. Vision Transformer Architecture

The architecture of the Vision Transformer is shown in figure 3.2. It is made up of a stack of $L$ identical encoder layers whose structure closely follows that of an encoder layer in the original Transformer. The encoder stack is fed a sequence of embeddings that are derived from the input image. The encoders process the embeddings and generate a set of encoded output embeddings which are used by downstream blocks for vision tasks. As is to be expected, the process of generating the embeddings varies from that used in NLP tasks and is discussed in detail in the

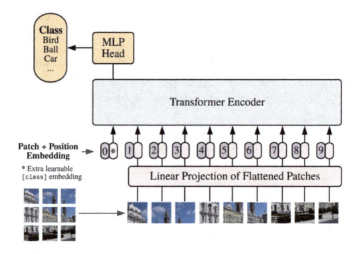

**Figure 3.2** Architecture of the Vision Transformer (from [10]).

following sections. While the structure of each encoder bears a close resemblance to the structure of the original Transformer encoder, important differences exist between the two architectures, and they are discussed in the following sections.

The following parameters are configurable in the ViT architecture - number of encoder layers ($L$), number of attention heads per encoder layer ($H$), length of embeddings or *hidden size* ($D$) and the number of nodes in the hidden layer of the MLP (see figure 1.6) inside each encoder ($M$). Different configurations of the ViT can be generated depending on the available computational power and the expected performance. They are discussed in section 3.2.3 below.

## 3.2.1. From Image to Embeddings

Figure 3.3 illustrates the process of generating input embeddings from an input image with $H$ rows, $W$ columns and $C$ components. The pre-processing stage consists of patch generation, patch flattening, token projection and position encoding. The projection and position encoding concepts are direct adaptations from the original Transformer architecture, whereas patch generation is specific to the ViT.

### 3.2.1.1. Patch Tokens and Embeddings

The original Transformer consumes tokens that are generated from words in a piece of input text, with a one-to-one correspondence between the words and tokens. The ViT also consumes a sequence of tokens, that in this case, come from an input image. Unlike a piece of text that can be split into words to generate tokens, an image does not have natural boundaries at which it can be partitioned. Instead, it is the computational complexity of the self-attention layer that dictates how an image will be converted into a sequence of tokens. Recall that since the self-attention layer computes pair-wise attention over all the input tokens, it has a quadratic computational complexity. That is, when the number of input tokens is $N$, the computational complexity is of the order of $O(N^2)$. This is why practical implementations of the original Transformer model place an upper bound on the number of input tokens.

This is also what makes it impractical to consider each pixel in an image as a separate input token to the ViT - the computational requirements would become intractable even for small images with a few thousand pixels. On the other hand, using the entire image as a single token is of no use either. To overcome this issue, the authors in [10] employed an old partitioning trick that has been used in several contexts in image processing – divide the image into non-overlapping 16×16 blocks (or patches) and use each such patch to generate an input token. That is, for an image of size $H \times W$ with $C$ components, each patch $\mathbf{I}_k$, has dimensions of 16×16× $C$ pixels (i.e., $\mathbf{I}_k \in \mathbb{R}^{16 \times 16 \times C}$). The number of patches that can be generated is therefore given by $N = \left\lceil \frac{H}{16} \right\rceil \left\lceil \frac{W}{16} \right\rceil$, where $\lceil . \rceil$ is the ceiling function. The ceiling function is used here because leftover patches at the right

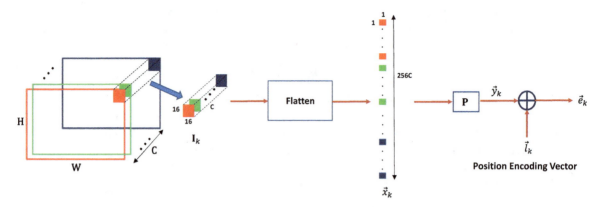

**Figure 3.3** Generation of an input embedding from an image patch.

and bottom edges of the image can be padded in order to generate complete 16×16 blocks. As shown in figure 3.3, the first pre-processing step is to unroll the image blocks to form a set of tokens. Every image patch $\mathbf{I}_k, 1 \le k \le N$, is *flattened* to yield a linear vector $\vec{x}_k$ with $256C$ components ($\vec{x}_k \in \mathbb{R}^{1\times256C}$). Although the collection of these flattened tokens from the entire image could be used directly, better performance was observed when these vectors were passed through a specialized linear projection layer prior to further processing.

The linear projection operation is a multiplication operation of each flattened patch with a projection matrix $\mathbf{P}$. In the case of the ViT, the most optimal projection matrix for each target task is learned during network training. The projection operation achieves two goals – the generated embeddings have properties that help in improving the performance of the ViT, and the flattened vectors are mapped to a lower-dimensional space which reduces the overall computational complexity. Each patch from the input image is projected to generate a *patch embedding* $\vec{y}_i$ of size $D$, which is known as the *hidden size* for the ViT. The architecture of the ViT is simplified and made scalable by having all the encoder layers operate on embeddings of this size.

The projection operation is identical to the projection of the tokens to word embeddings in the original Transformer. It can be similarly vectorized by collecting the flattened vectors for the entire image into a matrix (vector of vectors) $\mathbf{X}$ and generating a vector of patch embeddings $\mathbf{Y}$ using a single matrix operation.

$$\mathbf{Y}_{N\times D} = \begin{bmatrix} \vec{y}_1 \\ \vec{y}_2 \\ \vdots \\ \vec{y}_N \end{bmatrix} = \mathbf{X}_{N\times256C}\mathbf{P}_{256C\times D} = \begin{bmatrix} \vec{x}_1 \\ \vec{x}_2 \\ \vdots \\ \vec{x}_N \end{bmatrix} \mathbf{P}$$

A special embedding, in addition to these $N$ image patch embeddings, is generated and included in the input sequence. The idea of this special embedding, known as a *class embedding*, has been borrowed from the BERT architecture and its function is discussed in the next section.

### 3.2.1.2. Class Embedding

Every flattened input token $\vec{x}_k$, and hence every input embedding $\vec{y}_k$, carries information about a different local region of the image. These embeddings are used in the pair-wise attention computation and gather information about one another during this process. However, none of these embeddings can capture high-level information about the image as a whole. This is a problem because the purpose of the ViT is to generate a compact representation of the input image that can be used in downstream vision tasks such as object recognition and classification. If all the output embeddings generated by the ViT had to be used to gain an understanding at the image level, the downstream processing blocks would have to contend with a variable number of embeddings depending on the resolution of the input image. This is an undesirable dependency that should be avoided. On the other hand, always choosing just a fixed subset of the generated embeddings for further processing would introduce bias and could result in the under-representation of the information from certain parts of the image. This would obviously have a detrimental effect on the performance of the downstream blocks.

This problem is solved in the ViT using an additional learnable embedding that is fed to the encoder stack along with the patch embeddings. This additional embedding is known as a *class embedding* and its sole purpose is to accumulate global information about the image. It was named as such because the original application of the ViT was to classify the input image as belonging to one of several target categories. The class embedding ([**CLS**]) is prepended to the sequence of patch embeddings (it is always the first token in the input sequence) and initialized randomly during inference. It therefore does not contain any useful image information of its own. It has the same size as the patch embeddings (equal to the hidden size $D$) and is processed just like the other regular patch embeddings. Through the various encoder layers, the [**CLS**] embedding accumulates pieces of information about the different image patches using the self-attention mechanism.

In an image classification application, the output embedding from the encoder stack that corresponds to the class embedding is the only one that is processed further. This eliminates any bias towards any of the individual patches in the input image. The [**CLS**] output embedding is expected to have accumulated enough useful global information about the input image to be used as a representative token for all further processing.

### 3.2.1.3. Position Encoding

Unlike the original Transformer where deterministic positional information is added to each input token, the ViT uses learnable positional embeddings. The network learns the best way to encode positional data into the tokens based on the specific application. The embeddings could be one-dimensional (a single learnable embedding) or two-dimensional (two learnable embeddings). A one-dimensional embedding encodes the position of the token in raster-scan order and a two-dimensional embedding would encode the row and column indices. The latter choice seems like a natural fit since the image blocks lie on a grid, but it would also increase the number of network parameters. The authors in [10] decided to use 1D embeddings since no performance improvement was observed when 2D positional information was used instead. They also experimented with generating new position encoding vectors at the beginning of every encoder layer, but no benefit was seen in this approach either.

Note that a position encoding vector is generated for the class token as well. Referring to figure 3.3, the positional vectors $\vec{l}_k$ (of size $D$) are learned during training, one for each input token, and are added to the respective projected embeddings $\vec{y}_k, 0 \leq k \leq N$. This is possible since both the embeddings have identical dimensions. The resulting vectors become the input embeddings $\vec{e}_k = \vec{y}_k + \vec{l}_k, 0 \leq k \leq N$, to the ViT encoder stack. It was reported in [10] that the trained position embeddings for the patches along a single row or column show similarities, which indicates that the vectors successfully learn to represent the relative locations of the patches in the image.

### 3.2.2. Encoder Structure and Operations

The structure of each encoder layer in the ViT is shown in figure 3.4. The ViT encoder consists of a multi-head self-attention sub-layer followed by a fully connected MLP sub-layer, each of which applies pre-normalization to the input vectors. Both the sub-layers also have residual connections around the processing blocks that force the output vectors from these sub-layers to have the same size as their input vectors. As discussed earlier, this simplifies the design by enforcing a fixed hidden size $D$ for the embeddings across all the encoders.

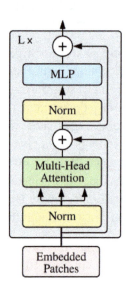

**Figure 3.4** Structure of an Encoder Layer in the Vision Transformer (from [10]).

The number of attention heads depends on the configuration of the ViT in use (see section 3.2.3). Within each attention head, the query, key and value projection matrices (**Q**, **K** and **V** respectively) are learned at training time. Just like in the original Transformer architecture, the outputs of the various attention heads are concatenated into a single vector and projected again using a learnable matrix to generate the final attention vector for an input embedding.

The basic ViT architecture is made up of a stack of 12 encoders, and the self-attention sub-layer within each encoder consists of 12 attention heads. The MLP sub-layer is like the FFN sub-layer in the original Transformer architecture (section 1.2.1.2.4) but uses the GELU activation layer, instead of RELU, in between the two linear layers. The first layer increases the size of the embedding to a configurable size of $M$ and the second layer brings the size back down to $D$.

The first encoder consumes the $N + 1$ positionally encoded input embeddings of size $D$ and generates an equal number of output embeddings of the same size. These outputs become the input embeddings to the second encoder in the stack, and so on.

The output embeddings from the final encoder in the stack consist of an embedding that corresponds to the input class embedding and $N$ other embeddings that correspond to the input image patch embeddings. In the original ViT, the output patch embeddings were discarded, and the output class embedding was further used for image classification.

As shown in figure 3.2, the output class embedding is passed through a MLP known as a *classification head*, whose structure is similar to that of the MLP used in the encoder layer. The differences lie in the use of tanh activation function in place of the GELU function and in the sizes of each fully-connected layer. Since this network is designed to generate unnormalized predictions over a task-specific number of image classes, the number of neurons in the output layer is equal to the number of target classes. As with the post-processing step of the decoder in the original Transformer architecture (section 1.2.2.2.3), the prediction scores generated by this MLP are passed through a softmax function to generate a probability distribution over the known classes.

### 3.2.3. Standard Configurations

The ViT architecture can be configured to meet the required performance and/or the available computational power. Three main configurations were proposed in the original ViT paper based on different combinations of values for the following parameters:

- Layers ($L$): The number of alternating pairs of multi-head self-attention and MLP sub-layers.
- Hidden size ($D$): The feature embedding dimension used by the encoder stack.
- Attention Heads ($A$): The number of attention heads in the self-attention sub-layer in each encoder.
- MLP Size ($M$): The size of the intermediate feature representation in the MLP block of each encoder.

Table 3.1 shows the three standard configurations, named ViT-Base (*ViT-B*), ViT-Large (*ViT-L*) and ViT-Huge (*ViT-H*), in increasing order of model complexity. The number of trainable parameters for each configuration is also listed in table 3.1. The advantage of a deeper ViT is that

| Model | Layers ($L$) | Attention Heads ($A$) | Hidden Size ($D$) | MLP Size ($M$) | #Parameters (Millions) |
|---|---|---|---|---|---|
| ViT-Base | 12 | 12 | 768 | 3072 | 86 |
| ViT-Large | 24 | 16 | 1024 | 4096 | 307 |
| ViT-Huge | 32 | 16 | 1280 | 5120 | 632 |

**Table 3.1** Configurations of the Vision Transformer.

the class embedding has the opportunity to gather deeper global information about the image. But this comes with increased computational requirements at both training and inference times.

Additionally, the size of the image patches is a configurable parameter. While the common sizes are 14×14 and 16×16, the patch size could be varied depending on the resolution of input image. Note that the patch size has a direct impact on the computational complexity since it controls the number of tokens that need to be processed (and computation is quadratic in the number of tokens). For a given image resolution, a smaller patch size would result in a larger number of tokens, and vice versa.

The ViT model configuration and the patch size are represented together using the *model/patch size* notation, where the size of the square patch is indicated by the length of its side. For example, *ViT-H/32* indicates that the ViT-Huge model is being used with a patch size of 32×32 pixels.

### 3.2.4. Fine-tuning and Performance

Image classification is a vital application in computer vision since it is often used as a gauge of the progress made in *representation learning*. Representation learning refers to techniques that enable a network or system to automatically discover the best image representations, from the input data, for a particular vision task. Progress in classification translates to improvements in other related vision tasks such as detection or segmentation. Networks that perform well on classification tasks are usually used as starting points in the development of networks for other tasks. This is also the case with the ViT, which originally targeted image classification, but was shown to perform well when fine-tuned for the target vision tasks from the VTAB benchmark [10].

When the ViT is fine-tuned for a new classification task, the classification head is replaced by a single linear layer that is initialized to zero and retrained. The size of this linear layer corresponds to the number of classes in the target task. Since the VTAB datasets include images with varying resolutions (in addition to the range of tasks), the ViT had to be fine-tuned to accommodate images of varied sizes. When the resolution of the target image is higher than the resolution used during pre-training, there are two options to overcome the mismatch - increase the patch size to keep the number of input tokens unchanged or keep the patch size unchanged and increase the number of tokens. In the former case, the ViT would have to be retrained to account for the larger patches

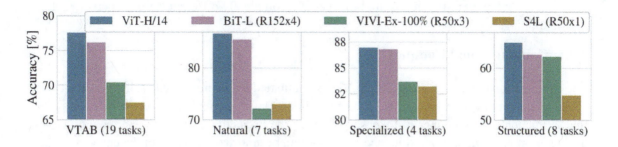

**Figure 3.5** ViT performance comparison with state-of-the-art CNNs (from [10]).

(the size of the embeddings, the hidden size of the MLP layers and the layer size of the classification head would all change). The preferred approach therefore is to keep the patch size the same as what was used during pre-training but increase the number of input tokens (the size of the embeddings, the hidden size of the MLP layers and the size of the classification head would all remain unchanged). While the architecture of the transformer blocks and the classifier do not need to be modified to process the increased number of tokens, the number of positional embeddings needs to be increased to match the number of tokens. It was found that the best results were obtained when 2D interpolation was applied to the pre-trained positional embeddings to generate the requisite number of embeddings for all the patches at the new higher image resolution [10].

In fine-tuning the ViT for other non-classification vision tasks, the classification head was replaced by a small task-specific CNN that was trained from scratch using a small subset of the task-specific data. The parameters of the encoder stack were also adjusted in this process in order to achieve optimal performance.

The *ViT-H/14* model was pre-trained on the large JFT-300M dataset, and its fine-tuned performance was evaluated on the 19-task VTAB test suite. For comparison, the state-of-the-art Resnet-based convolutional networks for transfer learning such as Big Transfer (BiT-L) [13], VIVI [14] and S4L [15] were also evaluated. The results are reproduced in figure 3.5, which compares the performance of the candidate models on the VTAB benchmark, and also provides a breakdown of the performance in each task category.

An alternative to using the output class token embedding for classification tasks is to use the output patch embeddings instead. An averaging operation, known in the literature as *global average pooling* (GAP), can be applied to each output patch embedding to generate a single number per image patch. The vector of values from the set of patch embeddings can be fed to an MLP classifier network that maps this vector to a probability distribution over the set of target classes. It was reported in [10] that this method produced results that were comparable to those obtained using the class embedding but that it required the use of a completely different set of hyperparameters during training.

### 3.2.5. Computational Complexity

The computational load in the case of the ViT is dominated by the multi-head self-attention layers since the number of operations in the rest of the model (layer normalization and MLP layers) is a linear function of the number of tokens. Moreover, the projection of the flattened input patches during pre-processing is a one-time operation that can be amortized over all of the encoders in the stack. Within the multi-head attention layer, computation is dominated by matrix multiplications. Therefore, in order to determine the computational complexity of the attention mechanism, we begin with the baseline fact that multiplying a matrix of size $d_1 \times d_2$ by a matrix of size $d_2 \times d_3$ requires $O(d_1 d_2 d_3)$ operations[1].

Table 3.2 lists each operation within an attention head and its corresponding computational complexity. $\mathbf{E}$ is the $N \times D$ matrix of flattened, projected and positionally encoded image patches (see figure 3.3), where $N$ is the number of patches and $D$ is the embedding size of the ViT. The query, key, value and attention vectors in each attention head are all assumed to have the same size of $\dfrac{D}{A}$ (where $A$ is the number of attention heads). The projection operation applied to the concatenated attention vectors results in a matrix of output embeddings $\mathbf{E}'$ with dimensions of

| Operation | Size of Matrix 1 | Size of Matrix 2 | Complexity |
|---|---|---|---|
| Compute Query Matrix $\mathbf{Q} = \mathbf{EW_Q}$ | $N \times D$ | $D \times D/A$ | $O(ND^2/A)$ per head |
| Compute Key Matrix $\mathbf{K} = \mathbf{EW_K}$ | $N \times D$ | $D \times D/A$ | $O(ND^2/A)$ per head |
| Compute Value Matrix $\mathbf{V} = \mathbf{EW_V}$ | $N \times D$ | $D \times D/A$ | $O(ND^2/A)$ per head |
| Compute Dot-product Matrix $\mathbf{QK^T}$ | $N \times D/A$ | $D/A \times N$ | $O(N^2 D/A)$ per head |
| Compute Softmax $\mathbf{S} = \mathbf{Softmax(QK^T)}$ | $N \times N$ | – | $O(N^2)$ per head |
| Compute Attention Matrix $\mathbf{R} = \mathbf{SV}$ | $N \times N$ | $N \times D/A$ | $O(N^2 D/A)$ per head |
| Project Concatenated Attention Matrix $\mathbf{E}' = \mathbf{BW_Z}$ | $N \times D$ | $D \times D$ | $O(ND^2)$ over A attention heads |
| Total (over A attention heads) | $O\left( A\left( \dfrac{3ND^2}{A} + \dfrac{2N^2 D}{A} + N^2 \right) + ND^2 \right) = O(4ND^2 + N^2(2D + A))$ | | |

**Table 3.2** Computational Complexity of a Multi-head Self-attention Layer in the Vision Transformer.

---

[1] Although more optimal algorithms exist, they result in meaningful savings only for sparse matrices and/or those with specific rank properties. Those conditions need not necessarily apply here.

$N \times D$. As expected, table 3.2 shows that the complexity of the multi-head self-attention layer is quadratic in the number of patches $N$, and by extension, the size of the image. This renders the ViT ill-suited for tasks that involve high-resolution images and/or pixel-level feature generation.

# 4. Shifted Window Transformers

The Vision Transformer architecture suffers from two drawbacks – it has a computational complexity that is quadratic in the image size (see table 3.2), and it can only generate a single feature map. The quadratic computational cost makes it prohibitive to use the ViT with high-resolution images. The generation of a feature map at a single resolution means that the ViT cannot be employed for tasks such as object detection and semantic segmentation that require a range of feature maps at various resolutions. These limitations of the ViT mean that the architecture cannot be used as a generic backbone network for vision applications. The backbone network is one that generates a range of generic feature maps independent of the specific end task. These feature maps can then be processed by task-specific mini-networks to achieve the end goal for each task.

Several modified architectures of the ViT have been suggested to overcome these limitations. While a few of these architectures reduce the computation cost, they still produce feature maps at a single resolution. Other alternative architectures produce hierarchical feature maps, but still have a quadratic computational complexity in the size of the image. A more recently proposed ViT-based architecture known as the *shifted window (Swin) transformer* [16] exhibits both of the desired characteristics - it produces a set of hierarchical feature maps that can be used for image recognition tasks at various scales (pixel-level in the case of semantic segmentation and image level for classification), and it provides a Transformer architecture whose computational cost is linear in image size.

The Swin transformer addresses the quadratic computational complexity with respect to image size by modifying the self-attention mechanism. In the process, it is also able to produce state-of-the-art results in several computer vision tasks by adding back a flavor of the localized processing characteristics of CNNs. The Swin Transformer has a hierarchical architecture that makes it an attractive backbone for a host of vision applications. Section 4.1 discusses the architecture of the Swin Transformer in detail, section 4.2 introduces an enhancement to this architecture to enable deeper models and section 4.3 delves into how this network can be efficiently trained as a generic backbone for computer vision tasks.

## 4.1. The Swin Architecture

Figure 4.1 shows the architecture of the smallest configuration of the Swin Transformer. This architecture consists of three identical stages of processing, preceded by a first stage that has a slightly different structure. The following notation is used in the rest of this chapter. Each partition

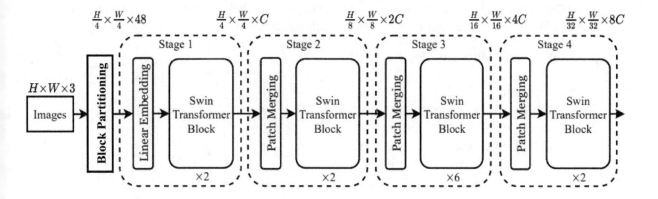

**Figure 4.1** Architecture of the Shifted Window Transformer (from [16]).

in the input image that is used to generate an input token is referred to as a *block* of the image. The smallest entity in a feature map is referred to as a *patch* and it could be an embedding generated from a token in the input image or an embedding in any of the feature maps that are generated after subsequent processing.

The input image is partitioned into blocks, flattened and fed to the first stage of processing. This stage is different since it is the only one to further apply a linear projection to the raw flattened input blocks to generate the corresponding tokens. As discussed in the following sections, each of the remaining stages instead merges 2×2 neighborhoods of patches in the input feature map to generate a spatially down-sampled version of the feature map. As indicated in figure 4.1, the processing stages consist of a varying number of Swin Transformer blocks and produce successively smaller feature maps with a proportionally higher number of components. The details of this architecture are discussed in the following sections.

### 4.1.1. Token Generation

Referring to figure 4.1, consider an input RGB image of size $H \times W$ pixels. The first step is to generate tokens from the input image. The block partition operation is similar to that performed by the ViT. The difference is that the image is partitioned into non-overlapping 4×4 blocks, instead of 16×16 blocks in the ViT, resulting in a total of $N = \left\lceil \frac{H}{4} \right\rceil \times \left\lceil \frac{W}{4} \right\rceil$ blocks for the image. Each 4×4×3 image block is then flattened to a linear vector with 48 components. The flattened vectors are linearly projected using an embedding matrix (learned during pre-training) to generate embeddings $x_i$, $0 \leq i \leq N - 1$, such that $x_i \in \mathbb{R}^{1 \times C}$. The number of components in each input embedding, $C$, is one of the configuration parameters used to generate Swin variants with varying complexity (see section 4.1.5). Note that unlike in the case of ViT, no positional encoding vector is added to the input embeddings. This is to account for the modified structure of the self-attention mechanism that will be described in more detail in the sections below. Instead, a relative positional bias is added to each token during the attention computation process (see section 4.1.3).

## 4.1.2. Swin Transformer Block

Every processing stage in the Swin architecture consists of an even number of Transformer blocks. This is because the modified attention mechanism requires that Swin Transformer blocks be used in pairs. Figure 4.2 shows the layers that make up such a pair of Swin Transformer blocks which can be considered to be *chained* together. The architecture of each individual block is similar to that of the original ViT except for the multi-head attention layer, which is replaced by either the *windowed multi-head attention (W-MSA)* layer or the *shifted windowed multi-head attention (SW-MSA)* layer as shown in figure 4.2. These new layers will be discussed in detail in the following sections. The rest of the

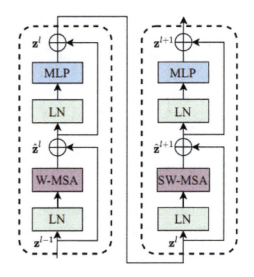

**Figure 4.2** Structure of a Chained Pair of Swin Transformer Blocks (from [16]).

architecture is identical to that of the ViT. Pre-normalization is applied in each block prior to both the self-attention and the MLP layers, and residual connections are present around each of these layers. The MLP layer consists of two fully-connected layers and the GELU activation function in between them.

### 4.1.2.1. Windowed Multi-head Self-attention

In the ViT, self-attention is computed over all the image embeddings in every encoder layer, and this results in a computational cost that is quadratic in the number of tokens. In the Swin Transformer architecture, the embeddings are partitioned into non-overlapping groups, and the self-attention computation for a group is limited to the embeddings within that group. Each group is processed independently to generate attention vectors for the embeddings in that group. This is the concept of the windowed multi-head self-attention (W-MSA) layer. In the W-MSA layer, the attention computation for an embedding is limited to a window of $M \times M$ contiguous embeddings in its spatial neighborhood. The window side length $M$ is programmable and set to a value of 7 by default in the original implementation in [16]. The number of attention windows is given by $\left\lceil \frac{N}{M^2} \right\rceil$, where $N$ is the number of image blocks. Figure 4.3 illustrates the concept of windowed self-attention for the case when $M = 2$ and $N = 36$. $x_{i,j}$ denotes the embedding that is generated from the image block at index $(i, j)$ and $a_{i,j}$ is the corresponding output attention vector. In this example, four output vectors are generated by computing self-attention over the four input embeddings within each attention window. Note that the windowed approach to self-attention still generates one attention vector output for every input embedding.

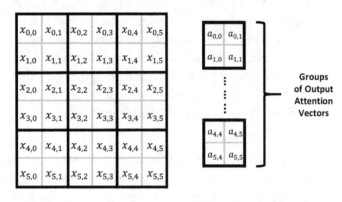

**Figure 4.3** Partitioning of Input Embeddings into Windows for Self-attention Computation.

The advantage of limiting the attention computation to a set of $M^2$ input embeddings is that it reduces the complexity of the multi-head self-attention layer from the original $O(4ND^2 + N^2(2D + A))$ as derived in table 3.2 to $O(4ND^2 + M^2(2ND + AN))$ as derived in table 4.1. In these computations, $N$ is the number of input tokens, $D$ is the length of the query/key/value vectors (and for simplicity, also the length of the flattened input vector. In the

| Operation | Size of Matrix 1 | Size of Matrix 2 | Complexity |
|---|---|---|---|
| Compute Query Matrix $\mathbf{Q} = \mathbf{EW_Q}$ | $N \times D$ | $D \times D/A$ | $O(ND^2/A)$ per head |
| Compute Key Matrix $\mathbf{K} = \mathbf{EW_K}$ | $N \times D$ | $D \times D/A$ | $O(ND^2/A)$ per head |
| Compute Value Matrix $\mathbf{V} = \mathbf{EW_V}$ | $N \times D$ | $D \times D/A$ | $O(ND^2/A)$ per head |
| Compute Dot-product Matrix $\mathbf{QK^T}$ (Repeated $N/M^2$ times) | $M^2 \times D/A$ | $D/A \times M^2$ | $O(M^4D/A)$ per window |
| Compute Softmax $\mathbf{S} =$ Softmax$(\mathbf{QK^T})$ (Repeated $N/M^2$ times) | $M^2 \times M^2$ | – | $O(M^4)$ per window |
| Compute Attention Matrix $\mathbf{R} = \mathbf{SV}$ (Repeated $N/M^2$ times) | $M^2 \times M^2$ | $M^2 \times D/A$ | $O(M^4D/A)$ per window |
| Project Concatenated Attention Matrix $\mathbf{E'} = \mathbf{BW_Z}$ | $N \times D$ | $D \times D$ | $O(ND^2)$ over A attention heads |
| Total (over A attention heads) | $O\left(A\left(\dfrac{3ND^2}{A} + \dfrac{N}{M^2}\left\{\dfrac{2M^4D}{A} + M^4\right\}\right) + ND^2\right)$ $= O(4ND^2 + M^2(2ND + AN))$ | | |

**Table 4.1** Computational Complexity of a Windowed Multi-head Self-attention Layer.

notation used earlier in figure 4.1, $D = C$), $A$ is the number of attention heads and $M$ is the side length of the attention window. The computational complexity of the MSA layer in the original ViT is fixed and is quadratic in the number of embeddings $N$, whereas the complexity of the W-MSA layer in the Swin is linear in the number of embeddings and scalable via the choice of the window side length $M$. Note that plugging in a value of $M^2 = N$ in table 4.1 yields the complexity of the ViT (from table 3.2) as expected. This is because, in that case, the W-MSA layer would compute attention over all the input embeddings and is therefore identical to the MSA layer in the original ViT.

Once the value of $M$ has been programmed, the same value is used in all the processing stages. Beginning with the second processing stage, each stage applies the self-attention window to the embeddings (patches) that are generated by the previous processing stage.

In addition to the central task of reducing computational complexity, the windowed approach to self-attention yields another important benefit. It introduces a measure of spatially localized processing in the attention computation that is missing in the traditional self-attention approach. Traditional CNNs benefit from the short-range correlations gathered from such localized processing whereas Transformers focus on figuring out long-range or global correlations through the self-attention mechanism. The introduction of localized contextual information into the attention vectors via the windowed self-attention approach has been seen to boost the performance of the Swin Transformer in a range of vision tasks [16].

### 4.1.2.2. Shifted-window Multi-head Self-attention

The main draw of the ViT architecture is its ability to produce feature maps that capture correlations from different regions of an image. This is achieved by computing the pair-wise attention over all the embeddings in the input image. The windowed approach of the Swin Transformer curtails the ability of the self-attention mechanism to gather long-range information since embeddings that belong to different windows are never processed together in the W-MSA layer. In order to compensate for this loss of non-local context, the Swin Transformer introduces the concept of *shifted attention windows* whereby the grid of windows is spatially displaced to generate new groups of patches for attention computation. This allows for the exchange of information between patches that belonged to different groups in the original window grid. The Swin Transformer architecture is therefore defined by pairs of chained Swin Transformer blocks, where the self-attention windows are spatially shifted between the first and second blocks. In the case of the first block, the windowing pattern is as shown in figure 4.3, and patches are partitioned into $M \times M$ windows beginning at the top-left of the image. The grid is then spatially shifted by $\left( \left\lfloor \frac{M}{2} \right\rfloor, \left\lfloor \frac{M}{2} \right\rfloor \right)$ patches in the output feature map before it is processed by the second Transformer block (in a chained pair). The self-attention layer in the second Swin Transformer block is therefore referred to as the *Shifted-window Multi-head Self-attention (SW-MSA)* layer (see figure 4.2). If the shifted windows were not used, attention would always be computed over the same

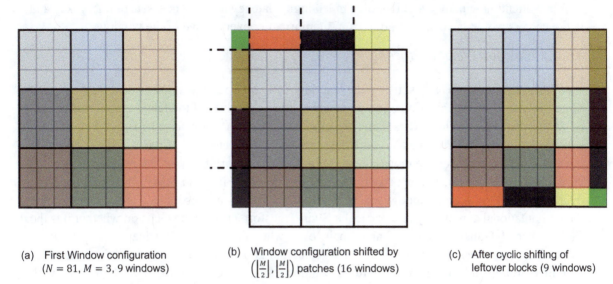

(a) First Window configuration
($N = 81$, $M = 3$, 9 windows)

(b) Window configuration shifted by $\left(\left\lfloor\frac{M}{2}\right\rfloor, \left\lfloor\frac{M}{2}\right\rfloor\right)$ patches (16 windows)

(c) After cyclic shifting of leftover blocks (9 windows)

**Figure 4.4** Shifted Windows for Attention Computation (patches of the same color belong to the same attention window).

limited set of patches down the processing chain. Window shifting allows for the propagation of information between patches from different windows, and results in attention vectors with richer overall representations.

Figure 4.4 illustrates the concept of shifted windows for a feature map with $N = 81$ total patches, arranged in a $9 \times 9$ grid, with an attention window side length of $M = 3$. In the figure, all the patches that belong to the same attention window are shown with the same color. Figure 4.4(a) shows the window grid used by the W-MSA layer in the first Swin Transformer of a chained pair. For the second Transformer in the pair, the grid is then displaced by $\left(\left\lfloor\frac{M}{2}\right\rfloor, \left\lfloor\frac{M}{2}\right\rfloor\right) = (1,1)$ tokens to generate the new attention windows shown in figure 4.4(b). It is obvious from figure 4.4(b) that this creates several additional attention windows (7 in this example), that are smaller than $M \times M$ in size, along the edges of the image. In general, the total number of attention windows increases from $\left\lceil\frac{H}{b}\right\rceil \times \left\lceil\frac{W}{b}\right\rceil$ to $\left(\left\lceil\frac{H}{b}\right\rceil + 1\right) \times \left(\left\lceil\frac{W}{b}\right\rceil + 1\right)$ as a result of the shift, where each patch is created from a $b \times b$ region in the input image of size $H \times W$. As described in the next section, these incomplete windows are intelligently combined for processing by the SW-MSA layer.

It was shown in [16] that the shifted window approach introduces important cross-connections between windows and is found to significantly improve the performance of the model in common vision tasks. It was also shown that this method is more hardware-friendly than, and required half the computation time of, the sliding window approach. In contrast to the shifted window approach, a sliding attention window would involve much higher latency because new sets of query, key and value vectors would have to be read in from memory after every move of the window.

### 4.1.2.3. Batched Window Processing

As illustrated in figure 4.4, shifting the window grid by half a window side length in each dimension results in the creation of new windows, along the edges of the feature map, that consist of fewer than $M^2$ patches. These smaller groups of patches are referred to as the *"leftover" windows*, and they could be padded with zeros to make complete $M \times M$ windows and passed to the attention layer. The attention layer would then mask off the padded regions during its computations. However, this approach has two drawbacks – it could lead to high computation overhead when the actual window size is small, and it creates an unbalanced architecture where the computational complexity of a particular Swin Transformer block depends on whether it is the first or second Transformer in a chained pair, even when the size of input feature map is fixed. The solution that was proposed in [16] is a technique known as *cyclic shifting* which involves wrapping around and combining the leftover windows to generate valid full $M \times M$ windows with no padding. The concept is illustrated in figure 4.4(c), where the leftover windows have been wrapped around (left-to-right, top-to-bottom and top-left to bottom-right) to generate a 3×3 grid of nine attention windows. Note that the number of windows is now the same as in figure 4.4(a) for the original grid. The new windows that are made up of the cyclically shifted sub-windows are referred to as *batched windows*.

Since batched windows are composed of several sub-windows that are not spatially adjacent in the feature map, a masking mechanism is employed in the SW-MSA layer to limit the self-attention computation to spatially adjacent sub-window. If this were not done, the nature of the attention computation would be different just for the patches that lie close to the edges of the input feature map. When computing attention for a sub-window within a batched window, all other sub-windows that are not from spatially adjacent regions in the original unshifted feature map are masked off. Note that this masked self-attention mechanism is turned off when processing the non-batched attention windows (the top-left 2×2 grid of attention windows in figure 4.4(c)).

The cyclic shifts are reversed once the attention computation has been completed, and the output patches are written back to their original unshifted locations in the output feature map.

The MLP layer in each Swin Transformer block up-samples each input embedding to generate a hidden representation, applies a non-linearity to the intermediate representation and then down-samples the processed vector to an output representation whose size is the same as that of the input. More specifically, the MLP module in any Swin transformer block at stage $s$ consists of an input layer with $C_s$ neurons, a fully-connected hidden layer with $4C_s$ neurons, a GELU non-linear activation function and an output layer with $C_s$ neurons.

### 4.1.3. Relative Position Bias

Positional information is important in processing data sequences because the order of inputs is important. Otherwise, the model would be invariant to any permutation of the elements of the sequence. The original Transformer for NLP tasks generated absolute position encodings using sinusoidal signals. The ViT made the absolute position embeddings learnable during training. It has been shown that Transformers benefit from using learnable *relative* positions between the input tokens rather than their absolute positions. Additionally, work in [17] showed that the performance of Transformer models in NLP tasks further improved when these relative positional vectors were included in the attention computation mechanism. The modified attention mechanism learns the best representations for the relative spatial distances between tokens based on the specific task at hand. Subsequently, this concept has been extended to and modified for Transformer architectures in vision tasks.

The concept of learnable relative position representations is illustrated in figure 4.5. Consider a one-dimensional sequence of 5 tokens, labelled $\vec{x}_0$ to $\vec{x}_4$ in figure 4.5(a). With respect to $\vec{x}_0$, token $\vec{x}_1$ is at a relative position of +1, $\vec{x}_2$ at a position of +2 and so on up to $\vec{x}_4$, which is at a position of +4. With respect to $\vec{x}_1$, token $\vec{x}_0$ is at a position of -1, $\vec{x}_2$ is at a position of +1 and so on. For $\vec{x}_4$, tokens $\vec{x}_0$ through $\vec{x}_3$ are at relative positions of -4, -3, -2 and -1 respectively. Every token is at a relative position of 0 with respect to itself. The range of relative positions for this example sequence is therefore -4 to +4. Consider the set of learned representations $\{\vec{y}_{-4}, \vec{y}_{-3}, \dots, \vec{y}_0, \vec{y}_{+1}, \dots, \vec{y}_{+4}\}$ that encode these distances. Then every token in the input sequence uses a different set of 5 (of the 9 total) learned position vectors to represent distances between itself and the other tokens in the sequence. The set of representations used by each token is shown in figure 4.5(b) under the corresponding token in figure 4.5(a). For example, token $\vec{x}_0$ uses $\vec{y}_{+1}$ through $\vec{y}_{+4}$ to represent the distances between itself and tokens $\vec{x}_1$ through $\vec{x}_4$ respectively, and $\vec{y}_0$ to

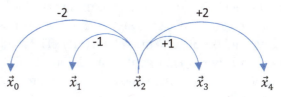

(a)   Relative Positions with respect to Token $\vec{x}_2$.

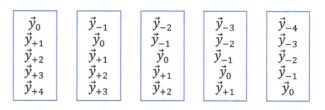

(b)   Sets of Relative Position Embeddings Used by Each Token.

**Figure 4.5**  Learned Relative Position Embeddings.

represent the zero distance to itself. Similarly, token $\vec{x}_2$ uses learned representations $\vec{y}_{-2}$ through $\vec{y}_{+2}$ to represent its distance from tokens $\vec{x}_0$ through $\vec{x}_4$ respectively. In general, each token would use as many relative position embeddings as there are tokens (say $t$) in the input sequence, and the total number of learned embeddings is equal to $2t - 1$.

The self-attention mechanism could then be modified to incorporate the relative distance between each pair of embeddings that it processes. For example, when computing the attention vector between the embeddings for the tokens $\vec{x}_1$ and $\vec{x}_4$, the query vector $\vec{q}_1$ is generated by suitably processing $\vec{x}_1$, and the key vector $\vec{k}_4$ and value vector $\vec{v}_4$ are generated by processing $\vec{x}_4$. The positional distance from $\vec{x}_1$ to $\vec{x}_4$ is +3, which is encoded by the learned relative position embedding $\vec{y}_{+3}$. The vector $\vec{y}_{+3}$ could be used to bias either the key or the value vector during the computation of the attention vector.

If $\vec{y}_{+3}$ is incorporated into the key vector, the attention vector between $\vec{x}_1$ and $\vec{x}_4$ would be computed                                                                                                      as

$$\vec{a}_{1,4} = Softmax\left( \frac{\vec{q}_1\left(\vec{k}_4 + \vec{y}_{+3}\right)^T}{\sqrt{l}} \right)\vec{v}_4.$$

On the other hand, if $\vec{y}_{+3}$ is used to bias the value vector, the computation would be given by

$$\vec{a}_{1,4} = Softmax\left( \frac{\vec{q}_1\vec{k}_4^T}{\sqrt{l}} \right)\left(\vec{v}_4 + \vec{y}_{+3}\right).$$

In both the equations, $l$ is the size of the query/key/value vector. The authors of [17] proposed a combination of these two schemes – that is, two learned relative position vectors, one added to the key vector and the other to the value vector. The resulting attention vector encodes the positional relationship between embeddings in addition to the semantic relationship between them. This additional piece of data was shown to improve the overall performance of self-attention architecture.

In the case of the Swin Transformer, a different type of relative position bias is included in the attention computation. In place of vector offsets for either the key or value vectors, a scalar bias is added to the input of the softmax function after the dot-product between the query and key vectors has been computed. That is, the attention vector computation takes the form of $\vec{a}_{i,j} = Softmax\left( \frac{\vec{q}_i\vec{k}_j^T}{\sqrt{l}} + \Delta_{i,j} \right)\vec{v}_j$, where $\Delta_{i,j}$ is the learned distance-based scalar bias value used when the patch $i$ generates the query, and patch $j$ generates the key and value vectors. Note that the term *patch* is used here as per its definition in section 4.1.

In a real-world vision application that uses the Swin architecture, we have a two-dimensional input sequence since each attention window consists of $M \times M$ patches. Following the discussion above, the range of distances along each axis is given by $[-M + 1, M - 1]$. Therefore, in the two-dimensional space, we need $(2M - 1)^2$ relative position biases in total to cover all the possible distances between any two patches in the attention window. In order to minimize the computation overhead involved in learning these bias parameters, a single $(2M - 1) \times (2M - 1)$ matrix of real numbers, denoted by $\widehat{\mathbf{B}} \in \mathbb{R}^{(2M-1)\times(2M-1)}$, is learned once and reused across all the attention windows in the input feature map and all the attention heads in every self-attention layer. For each query patch $\vec{x}_i, 0 \leq i < M^2$, the other patches in the attention window are located at a range of distances for which the learned bias values occupy a contiguous sub-matrix, denoted by $\mathbf{B}_i \in \mathbb{R}^{M \times M}$, of the larger matrix $\widehat{\mathbf{B}}$. This sub-matrix $\mathbf{B}_i$ is then used in the attention computation for the patch $\vec{x}_i$. It is obvious that a different sub-matrix is used for each patch in the attention window.

The relative position bias matrix learned during pre-training can be adapted to larger attention window sizes that might be encountered during fine-tuning. This is achieved by interpolating the entries in the bias matrix to generate the desired number of bias values. It was reported in [16] that significant performance gains were achieved by using a scalar bias when compared with methods that used regular self-attention or those that used an embedding to encode the absolute patch location within the attention window. The use of a relative position bias introduces a level of translation invariance that is a characteristic of CNNs and is missing in the original ViT and plays a role in boosting the performance of the Swin architecture in dense recognition tasks.

## 4.1.4. Hierarchical Feature Maps

The Swin Transformer addresses the need for hierarchical feature maps in order to enable a wide range of vision tasks. The Swin architecture is divided into processing stages, where each successive stage generates a feature map with a smaller resolution. From one stage to the next, the feature maps are down-sampled by a factor of 4 spatially (factor of 2 each along the rows and columns) and up-sampled by a factor of 2 in the number of channels. The Swin Transformer implements spatial down-sampling using a convolution-free technique known as *patch merging*, which is the first layer of every processing stage starting with the second stage (see figure 4.1).

Figure 4.6 illustrates the operations involved in merging patches between processing stages $s$ and $s + 1$ in the Swin architecture. Each patch in the input feature map $F_s$ is assumed to have $C_s$ components. This feature map with spatial dimensions of $H_s \times W_s$ is first partitioned into non-overlapping 2×2 regions of patches. As shown in figure 4.6, the four patches in each non-overlapping 2×2 region are concatenated in the depth direction to yield a single embedding with $4C_s$ components. The resulting intermediate feature map now has dimensions of $\left(\frac{H_s}{2}, \frac{W_s}{2}, 4C_s\right)$. This intermediate feature map is then passed through a two-layer fully-connected linear projection network (with no non-linear activation function) to generate an output feature map $F_{s+1}$ with dimensions $\left(\frac{H_s}{2}, \frac{W_s}{2}, 2C_s\right)$. The weight matrix and bias vector for this fully-connected network are also learned during pre-training.

In order to produce a hierarchical representation, the number of patches in the feature map is reduced as the network gets deeper. Referring to figure 4.1, processing begins with an input image

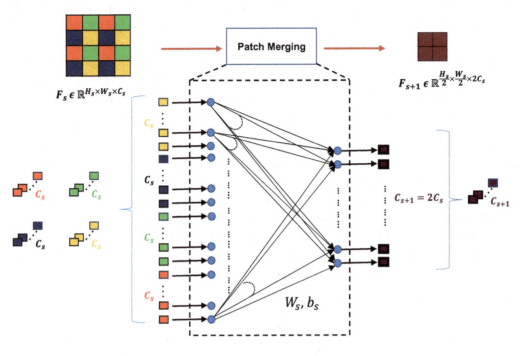

**Figure 4.6** Feature Map Down-sampling (2×2) via Patch Merging between Processing Stages $s$ and $s + 1$.

of size $H \times W \times 3$ pixels, which yields $\frac{H}{4} \times \frac{W}{4}$ tokens. The first processing stage then generates a feature map of patches with a dimension of $\frac{H}{4} \times \frac{W}{4} \times C$, where $C$ is the number of components in the latent representation (embedding) generated for each token in the first processing stage. The patch merging layer at the front of the second stage concatenates the features of each group of 2×2 neighboring patches and applies a linear projection to the resulting $4C$-dimensional latent representation. This generates an intermediate feature map with one-fourth the number of patches and twice the number of channels ($2C$). This new feature map is processed by the second stage, whose output is a feature map with dimensions of $\frac{H}{8} \times \frac{W}{8} \times 2C$. Similarly, the third processing stage generates a feature map with dimensions of $\frac{H}{16} \times \frac{W}{16} \times 4C$, and the fourth stage outputs a feature map of size $\frac{H}{32} \times \frac{W}{32} \times 8C$. These stages jointly produce a set of hierarchical representations in which the resolutions of the feature maps match those from popular CNNs (such as ResNets) that are commonly used as vision backbones. The Swin architecture can therefore conveniently replace these CNNs as a generic backbone network for vision tasks.

As an example, consider the task of image classification, to be performed on a 224×224 input image, using the Swin Transformer. Based on the discussion above, if the hidden representation for each token has 96 components, the fourth processing stage would generate a feature map with dimensions of $\frac{224}{32} \times \frac{224}{32} \times (8 * 96)$, which is 49 embeddings with 768 components each. This would be followed by an average pooling layer which would generate a single spatial average value for each component in the feature map. This generates a vector of 768 components, which can be fed to a simple classification head. The output from the classification head is a probability distribution over all the possible classes. The most probable class is then assigned to the input image.

The Swin Transformer was seen to match or beat the performance of the data-efficient version of the ViT (known as DeiT) and the state-of-the-art CNN models when tested on a broad set of representative vision tasks - image classification on the ImageNet-1K dataset, object detection on the COCO dataset, semantic segmentation on the ADE20K dataset, and video action recognition on the Kinetics-400 dataset. Chapter 5 contains detailed discussions on the use of the Swin Transformer model for a range of common vision tasks.

## 4.1.5. Standard Configurations

The configuration of a Swin Transformer is defined by the following five parameters:

- The number of components in the latent (hidden) representation of each input token ($C$)

- The number of Swin Transformer blocks in each of the four stages indicated as an ordered set ($\{N_1, N_2, N_3, N_4\}$)

Table 4.2 shows the parameter values for the four standard configurations known as Tiny (*Swin-T*), Small (*Swin-S*), Base (*Swin-B*) and Large (*Swin-L*). A constant size of 32 for each query/key/value vector is used across the stages for all the configurations. A constant attention window side length (set to $M = 7$ by default) is used across all the layers within each configuration. In each configuration, the MLP layer within each Swin block first upscales the feature vector by a factor of 4 (known as the expansion factor) in the hidden layer and then down-

| Model | #Components in Hidden Representation ($C$) | #Swin Blocks in Stage 1 ($N_1$) | #Swin Blocks in Stage 2 ($N_2$) | #Swin Blocks in Stage 3 ($N_3$) | #Swin Blocks in Stage 4 ($N_4$) |
|---|---|---|---|---|---|
| Swin-T | 96 | 2 | 2 | 6 | 2 |
| Swin-S | 96 | 2 | 2 | 18 | 2 |
| Swin-B | 128 | 2 | 2 | 18 | 2 |
| Swin-L | 192 | 2 | 2 | 18 | 2 |

**Table 4.2** Configurations of the Swin Transformer.

scales the intermediate feature vector by a factor of 4 to output a feature vector with the same size as the input feature vector. With these settings, the Swin-B configuration has similar complexity to the ViT-B model, and the Swin-T, Swin-S and Swin-L configurations have 0.25, 0.5 and 2.0 times the complexity in comparison, respectively.

## 4.2. Swin Transformer Version 2

Since the introduction of the original Transformer architecture, significant strides have been made in the NLP field in terms of the performance of language models. As discussed in chapter 2, these models have become powerful enough to learn from relatively small sets of training samples (i.e., few-shot capability), thus coming close to mimicking human ability. These improvements have been linked directly to the explosion in the sizes of these new models. Language models with tens of billions of parameters are common and have been deployed successfully.

On the other hand, vision models have lagged behind in terms of model size with the largest models made up of about 1 or 2 billion parameters. One of the reasons for this is that deeper Transformer models for vision tasks suffer from instability during training [18]. Studies have shown that there are three main issues with training very deep vision models.

1. The values of certain signals could grow out of control and result in instability during training. This is caused by the residual connections adding back the signal to the processed output in the main branch. The magnitude of the signal could continue to increase with model depth, depending on the model and the specific input, and at some point, cause the training run to crash.
2. The resolutions of the images used during inference tend to be different from those used during training. This is especially true when the trained network is employed as a backbone for a range of vision tasks. This necessitates the adaptation of the trained parameters such as the relative position bias matrix to be interpolated based on the new window sizes. This has been seen to lead to sub-optimal performance as well.
3. It takes a very large amount of labelled data to effectively train large vision models. For example, scaled-up versions of the ViT were trained on the JFT dataset that consisted of 300 million to 3 billion images. Training larger models would require much larger datasets of labelled images, and sourcing image datasets of this magnitude is an obstacle.

The Swin Transformer Version 2 (or Swin V2) is a modified Swin architecture that aims to overcome the first two issues mentioned above. Figure 4.7 shows the architecture of Swin V2 and highlights (in red) the changes from the original Swin architecture. The four differences between the two models are in the use of:

- post-normalization in place of pre-normalization
- scaled cosine attention in place of dot-product attention

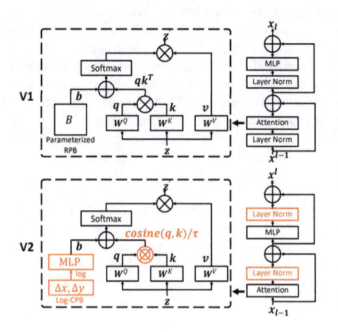

**Figure 4.7** Comparison of Swin Transformer Architectures (from [18]).

- logarithmic (instead of linear) relative positions between patches, and,

- a small learned two-layer MLP to dynamically generate the final relative position bias values from the logarithmic relative position inputs.

The following sections describe how these modifications alleviate the listed issues with training deep vision Transformer models. The improvements can be classified into two broad categories – model capacity enhancement and better adaptability to varying attention window sizes.

The question of how to efficiently train vision Transformer models using relatively small unlabeled datasets is addressed by a framework known as *masked image modeling* (*MIM*) which is discussed in detail in section 4.3.

## 4.2.1. Model Capacity

Model capacity refers to the size of the model in terms of depth and the number of learnable parameters. NLP models have benefited from having billions of learnable parameters, while vision models have lagged behind due to issues with training large models. The following two modifications were introduced in the Swin V2 architecture to address this problem.

### 4.2.1.1. Post-normalization

ViTs apply layer normalization to the signal before it is processed by either the self-attention layer or the MLP layer in each Transformer block. The creators of ViT referenced learnings from the NLP domain where it was observed that the use of post-normalization results in large signal gradients after the residual signal was combined with the attention vector in the self-attention layers. This necessitated the use of a small learning rate during training to ensure stability, but this led to slower convergence and longer training times.

However, the architects of Swin V2 relied on the observation that using pre-normalization in deep Swin Transformers for vision causes the actual signal values (and not the gradients) to explode during training and limits the depth of the model that can be successfully trained. In the Swin architecture (and in the ViT), the signal is amplified when it is processed either by a self-attention layer or an MLP layer. It is easy to see that since layer normalization is applied prior to this processing step, there is no mechanism to rein in the amplitude of the processed signal before it is combined with the original input signal via the skip connection. The combination further amplifies the signal which is again sent through the skip connection in the next layer to be combined with another amplified version of itself, and so on. This could easily cause the signal magnitude to blow up even in a medium-sized network.

The Swin V2 architecture employs post-normalization to overcome this issue. As seen in figure 4.7, layer normalization is applied after the signal has passed through either a self-attention layer or an MLP layer. This ensures that a normalized signal with a much smaller amplitude is carried forward via the skip connections. This limits the build-up in the signal values in the deeper layers during training and has been shown to help alleviate the problem of training instability.

### 4.2.1.2. Scaled Cosine Attention

The self-attention layer in the Swin architecture computes the attention weights using the dot products between the query and key vectors. However, since the Swin V2 architecture uses post-normalization, it was seen that in the deeper layers of large vision models, the dot-product attention weights were usually dominated by a small number of query-key pairs. That is, a few large-valued query and key vectors had an outsized influence on the composition of the final attention vector. This meant that the model was ignoring other potentially useful correlations because the computed attention weights had a skewed distribution. This problem can be resolved by using some form of weight normalization based on the strengths of the vectors.

The Swin V2 architecture achieves this by replacing the dot-product attention with a scaled cosine function, as shown below. The cosine attention weight between two vectors is given by their dot-product divided by the product of their magnitudes.

$$cos(\vec{q}, \vec{k}) = \frac{\vec{q}\vec{k}^T}{\|\vec{q}\|\|\vec{k}\|}$$

$$Similarity(\vec{q}_i, \vec{k}_j) = \frac{cos(\vec{q}_i, \vec{k}_j)}{\tau} + \delta_{i,j},$$

where $\delta_{i,j}$ is the relative position bias between patches $i$ and $j$, $\tau > 0.01$ is a scalar which is learned independently by each attention head in each encoder layer. The cosine function generates a bounded output that is independent of the magnitudes of the input vectors, and thus also plays a significant part in restricting the signal value in deeper models.

It was reported in [18] that the two modifications to the Swin architecture that were discussed above not only make the training process more stable but also lead to an improvement in the performance of vision Transformer models of all sizes.

## 4.2.2. Window Resolution

The last two modifications focus on improving the accuracy of the relative positional bias values with varying attention window sizes. This is an important aspect of utilizing the Swin Transformer architecture as a backbone for vision tasks. The variation in the attention window size could result from either a change in the resolution of the input image or from using a different attention window size in a downstream vision task, or both. Many vision tasks such as object detection and semantic segmentation require high resolution input images or large attention windows. The common practice is to perform a bi-cubic interpolation of the pre-trained position bias matrix to adapt to the larger window sizes. However, the performance of this approach, known as *parameterized position bias*, has been found to be sub-optimal, and the Swin V2 architecture addresses this problem with two specific enhancements. It was shown that these enhancements, known together as *log-spaced continuous position bias (log-CPB)*, play a significant role in improving the performance of the Swin V2 model when compared to the Swin model, and in enabling its use as a generic backbone for vision tasks. The two features that make up log-CPB enhancements are log-spaced coordinates and continuous position bias values.

### 4.2.2.1. Log-spaced Coordinates

The Swin V2 architecture uses a modified representation for the distances between the patches in the feature map. In the original Swin Transformer, distances between patches are expressed linearly. That is, the distance from a patch at location (3, 2) to a patch at location (1, 6) would be represented simply as $\Delta X = 4$ and $\Delta Y = -2$. The Swin V2 architecture instead represents distances in logarithmic space, as shown below.

$$\Delta\hat{X} = sign(\Delta X)\ln(1 + |\Delta X|)$$

$$\Delta\hat{Y} = sign(\Delta Y)\ln(1 + |\Delta Y|)$$

In this space, the distance between the two patches in the example above would be represented as $\Delta\hat{X} = 1.609$ and $\Delta\hat{Y} = -1.099$. This changes the relative position representation from an integer to a real number, and therefore changes the specifics of the bias estimation. Due to the nature of the logarithm function, the range of position values becomes compressed and the effect of large variations in window sizes is minimized. This brings down the scaling ratio when the inference window size is much larger than the pre-trained window size, and results in more accurate interpolated bias values. As discussed in the next section, this change also enables the computation of biases for arbitrary coordinate ranges using a simple MLP network.

### 4.2.2.2. Continuous Relative Position Bias

In the original Swin Transformer, the relative position bias matrix is computed during pre-training for a particular attention window size and is interpolated using bicubic interpolation for any other window size that might be used at inference time. It was shown that this causes sub-optimal performance, and therefore the architecture in the Swin V2 architecture was modified to address this issue.

Instead of using a static relative position bias matrix that is generated during pre-training, the bias values in the Swin V2 architecture are generated dynamically using a simple MLP which consists of a configurable hidden layer and uses the ReLU activation function. A common implementation of this network is illustrated in figure 4.8, where the inputs to the network are the distances between the patches in logarithmic space $(\Delta\hat{X}, \Delta\hat{Y})$, and the output is an array of positional bias values, one per attention head. Allowing the network to learn to generate an independent bias value for each attention head should potentially help in improving the overall performance of the model. Recall that, as was the case with the parameterized bias matrix, the same bias

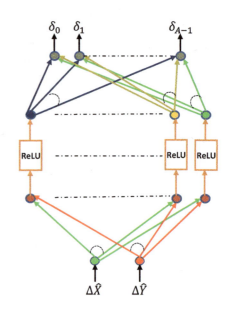

**Figure 4.8** Network to Generate Relative Position Bias Values ($A$ = number of attention heads).

values are used across all the layers. The advantage of using the log-spaced co-ordinates is a compression of the range of relative positions that are used to train the MLP.

Since the MLP consumes an arbitrary pair of coordinates, it can be fine-tuned across any range of attention window sizes. Additionally, in order to ease the computational burden during inference, the MLP could be used to pre-compute the bias matrices for all the downstream tasks with known window sizes. The appropriate bias matrix can then be employed for the corresponding task. This is similar to the parameterized bias approach but avoids the performance hit due to the interpolated bias values.

It was reported in [18] that using log-CPB by itself improved the performance of the Swin-T Transformer when compared to using either linear coordinates with the CPB approach or the parameterized relative position bias approach. Visualization of the learned relative position bias

| Model | #Components in Hidden Representation ($C$) | #Swin Blocks in Stage 1 ($N_1$) | #Swin Blocks in Stage 2 ($N_2$) | #Swin Blocks in Stage 3 ($N_3$) | #Swin Blocks in Stage 4 ($N_4$) | #Parameters (Millions) |
|---|---|---|---|---|---|---|
| SwinV2-T | 96 | 2 | 2 | 6 | 2 | 28 |
| SwinV2-S | 96 | 2 | 2 | 18 | 2 | 50 |
| SwinV2-B | 128 | 2 | 2 | 18 | 2 | 88 |
| SwinV2-L | 192 | 2 | 2 | 18 | 2 | 197 |
| SwinV2-H | 352 | 2 | 2 | 18 | 2 | 658 |
| SwinV2-G | 512 | 2 | 2 | 42 | 4 | 3000 |

**Table 4.3** Configurations of the Swin V2 Transformer.

matrices [18] shows that using the log-CPB scheme generates spatially smoother biases when compared to the other two bias schemes. A positional bias value is in effect a distance penalty that is used to modify the output of the softmax function depending on the distance between patches. In order to produce consistent results, it is therefore desirable for this penalty function to vary smoothly with distance and to not have discontinuities. The log-CPB scheme was found to be the best-performing candidate in this regard.

### 4.2.3. Standard Configurations

The standard configurations of the Swin V2 Transformer are shown in table 4.3, along with the number of learnable parameters for each model. The first four models, SwinV2-T through SwinV2-L, have the same complexity as their corresponding Swin V1 configurations. SwinV2-H (*Swin V2-Huge*) and SwinV2-G (*Swin V2-Giant*) are specific to the Swin V2 architecture and are orders of magnitude more complex than the other models. One architectural note here is that in both of these models, a layer normalization block is inserted into the signal path once every six layers to further restrict the magnitude of the signal.

Training the SwinV2-G model with 3 billion parameters was made possible due to the feature enhancements that were directed towards limiting the signal magnitude. As reported in [18], the fact that this model can also train on image resolutions of the order of 1536x1536 pixels is proof of the effectiveness of the log-CPB feature. The SwinV2-G Transformer was seen to beat the performance of the Swin V1 Transformer models and the corresponding state-of-the-art CNN models when used as a backbone network for image classification, object detection, semantic segmentation and video action recognition.

## 4.3. Training Vision Transformers – SimMIM

As discussed in chapter 2, Transformers for NLP tasks can be trained using a paradigm known as *masked language modeling (MLM)*. The distinct advantage of the MLM approach is that the language model can be pre-trained for a variety of downstream tasks using *unlabeled* data. The MLM training paradigm consists of two stages - pre-training and fine-tuning. During pre-training, the model is trained on unlabeled data over different pre-training tasks. For fine-tuning, the model is first initialized with the pre-trained parameters, and all of the parameters are fine-tuned using task-specific labeled data for each task. Each downstream task has separate fine-tuned models, even though they are initialized with the same pre-trained parameters.

MLM begins with a curated language training corpus, from which sequences of tokens are generated out of either individual words or full sentences. The choice depends on whether the pre-training task involves predicting words (as in sentence completion) or full sentences (as in question answering). A small percentage of these input tokens are then masked off before they are fed to the model. Masking involves replacing a token with either a random token or a pre-determined special mask token. The training process then involves teaching the model to predict the token that has been masked off using the context of the unmasked tokens. The predicted output representation for each masked token is passed through a simple decoder, and the decoded token passed through a softmax layer over the input vocabulary to determine the word or sentence that it represents. Finally, the cross-entropy loss between the predicted and actual text is used as the error function to be minimized via backpropagation.

The same idea can be extended to training vision Transformers using *masked image modeling (MIM)*, where regions of the input image are masked off. The vision Transformer is then tasked with regenerating the masked regions using the context of the rest of the image. A loss function is constructed to determine the accuracy of the reconstruction and used to train the Transformer iteratively.

Several complex system designs have been proposed in the literature to train vision Transformers in general. The complexities are related to the choice of the following four major training components:

- Masking strategy - Given an input image, this component involves the choice of the area to be masked and the masking of the selected area. The transformed image after masking is used as the input to the model.
- Encoder architecture – The encoder generates latent feature representations, for the masked regions of the image, which are used to predict the masked areas. The MIM framework can be used to train any of the vision Transformer architectures – ViT, SwinV1, Swin V2 etc.

- Prediction head - This is the "decoder" portion of the training configuration since it takes in the latent feature representations from the encoder to generate output vectors corresponding to the masked regions in the input image.
- Prediction target – This design component determines the form of the missing image data and therefore the form of the predicted image data as well. The prediction target can be regions of either raw pixel values or some transformed version of the raw pixels. Since the training process requires a loss function to be minimized, this choice also dictates the nature of the loss function.

Several options have been proposed in the literature for each of these components. For the masking strategy, in addition to the spatial size of the mask, a range of masking methods such as image patch-aligned random masking, square central region masking, movable random masking and block-based masking have been proposed in the literature. Note that in this section, the term "patch" refers to a spatial region of the input image. For the prediction head, the choices range from a convolution neural network to a more complex Transformer decoder. For the prediction target, one could use raw pixel values, or some form of color clustering or component-based color discretization. This also dictates the choice of the loss function such as cross-entropy classification loss, or $\ell_1$ or $\ell_2$ regression losses.

A simplified masked image modeling training framework for vision Transformers, named *SimMIM*, was presented in [19]. The significance of the term "simplified" here is that the authors in [19] have been able to show that picking a low complexity option for each training component still results in an overall training strategy that is very effective. Additionally, this framework operates with unlabeled image data and thereby eliminates the need to continuously generate or gather new labeled image data to train data-hungry vision models as they grow in scale.

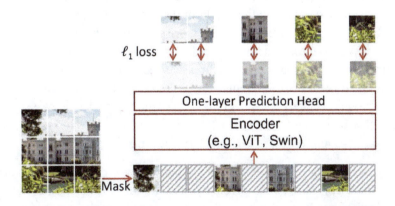

**Figure 4.9** Architecture of the SimMIM Training Framework (from [19]).

Figure 4.9 shows the components of the SimMIM training framework. The effectiveness of training a model with a combination of design choices was quantified in [19] by measuring the performance of the final pre-trained model when it was fine-tuned for four representative downstream vision tasks - image classification, object detection, semantic segmentation and video action recognition. Several design combinations were used to pre-train vision Transformers such as ViT-B, Swin-B, Swin-L, SwinV2-H, and SwinV2-G, and the performances of these models on the tasks listed above were used to guide the final design choices.

SimMIM employs a patch-aligned random masking strategy, which means that the size of a mask is an integer multiple of the size of an input patch. This makes sense since image patches are the basic processing units of vision Transformers. The patches to be masked are chosen randomly according to a masking ratio. The size of the mask and the masking ratio determine the performance of the trained network. It was found that for a mask size of 32×32, this approach yields competitive performance for a wide range of masking ratios (10%-70%). On the other hand, for a small mask patch size of 8, the masking ratio needs to be as high as 80% for good performance. A mask size of 32×32 pixels and a masking ratio of 0.6 were adopted as the default.

For the prediction head, several choices with varying computational complexity were tested. It was found that an extremely lightweight prediction head, consisting of a single linear layer, was able to achieve similar or slightly better fine-tuning performance than those of heavier prediction heads over a range of target image resolutions from 12×12 pixels through 192×192 pixels. Moreover, it was seen that although more complex prediction heads can lead to more generalized learning, this capability does not benefit downstream tasks after fine-tuning. The final training framework in figure 4.9 therefore consists of a single linear layer as the prediction head. The use of an extremely lightweight prediction head brings about a significant increase in speed, and a sizeable reduction in the computational complexity, of the pre-training process.

The simplest prediction target to use is the raw pixel values and is therefore chosen in SimMIM. The vision model is trained to predict the values of the pixels in the masked regions of the image. Since the Swin Transformer generates a down-sampled feature map after the last processing stage, the feature vector is passed through a linear layer (prediction head) that maps the vector to a region in the original input image. As an example, for a mask size of 32×32 pixels in the input image, the 32x down-sampled feature vector from each masked region (in the input image) at the output of the fourth processing stage of a Swin Transformer (see figure 4.1) is passed through a linear layer that generates 3072 output values. These 3072 values are rearranged to generate the prediction for the corresponding 32×32×3 patch of RGB pixels in the input image.

A simple $\ell_1$-regression loss function is computed between the predicted pixels and the original pixels. That is, the error function is given by sum of the absolute differences between the corresponding predicted and actual pixel values. The sum of squared errors was also considered

($\ell_2$-loss) but did not provide any improvement in performance. Therefore, the $\ell_1$ loss was retained since it further reduces the computational complexity of the framework.

As a result of these choices, the SimMIM framework minimizes the computational power required for, and eliminates the use of labelled data in, training large vision models. At the same time, the SimMIM approach has been shown to be very effective in training vision Transformers at a wide range of scales – from ViT-B with around 100 million parameters to a SwinV2-G Transformer with 3 billion parameters. Specifically, a SwinV2-G model that was pre-trained on the ImageNet-22K-ext dataset was able to meet or beat the state-of-the-art performance on image classification, object recognition, semantic segmentation and video action recognition. The fact that the unlabeled ImageNet-22K-ext dataset has $1/40^{th}$ the size of the previously used JFT-3B dataset shows that the SimMIM framework can play a significant role in eliminating the need for large, labelled datasets to train ever-growing vision models.

# 5. Swin Transformers in Action

The Swin architecture was designed to be used as a generic backbone network for a range of vision tasks. In fact, as discussed in [16], the dimensions of the hierarchical feature maps in the standard Swin Transformer (Swin-T) match those that are generated by popular CNN backbones such as ResNets. This chapter explores several network architectures that utilize the Swin architecture as a backbone network to enable common vision tasks.

## 5.1. Image Classification

Image classification is one of the simplest vision tasks in terms of computational complexity. Although the Swin Transformer backbone produces a hierarchical feature map, the task of image classification can be accomplished using just the feature map generated by the last processing stage in the Swin architecture. Image classification is performed by applying a global average pooling layer on the output feature map of the last stage, followed by a linear classifier. The sequence of operations is shown in figure 5.1. The output of the final processing stage of the Swin Transformer backbone is a feature map of size $H_F \times W_F \times C_F$, where $C_F$ is the number of channels in the feature map. The global average pooling operation converts the $H_F \times W_F \times C_F$ feature map into a $1 \times 1 \times C_F$ vector by replacing each of the input channels by the average value of that channel. The resulting vector is fed to a linear classifier that outputs a logit vector whose size is equal to the number of possible image classes. The logit vector is then passed through a softmax

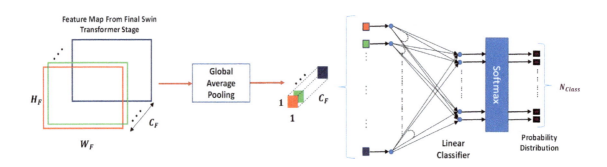

**Figure 5.1** Image Classification using a Swin Transformer Backbone.

layer to generate a probability distribution over the image classes. The class with the highest probability is assigned to the input image.

According to [16], the classification accuracy with this method is on par with that obtained by processing the class token output vector from a ViT using a classification head. The architecture in figure 5.1 can be trained using the cross-entropy loss function, just like a simple linear classifier would be, with the difference in this case being that a single vector generated from the output of the backbone network is used as the input to the classifier in place of the original input image.

## 5.2. Object Detection and Segmentation

The original Swin Transformer paper [16] evaluated the use of the Swin backbone for tasks such as object detection, instance segmentation and semantic segmentation. Instance segmentation extracts the different objects of interest in an image and assigns a different label to every instance of every object class. On the other hand, semantic segmentation is the task of assigning a class label to every pixel in the input image. In contrast to instance segmentation, semantic segmentation assigns identical labels to all the objects in the image that belong to the same class. Instance segmentation is challenging because it requires the correct detection of all objects in an image while also precisely segmenting each instance. It therefore combines the characteristics of object detection, where the goal is to classify every individual object and localize it using a bounding box, and semantic segmentation, where the goal is to classify each pixel into a fixed set of categories without differentiating between object instances.

In [16], the Swin Transformer backbone was evaluated with the Mask R-CNN network for object detection and instance segmentation, and with UPernet for semantic segmentation. Irrespective of the backbone used (CNNs or Swin), performance gains have been seen when the pyramid of the hierarchical feature maps was pre-processed by a feature pyramid network (FPN) before it is used for segmentation or object detection. The FPN, Mask R-CNN and UPerNet architectures are introduced in the following sections, along with the details of how the Swin Transformer backbone fits into these frameworks.

### 5.2.1. Feature Pyramid Network

The feature pyramid network [20] is a convolutional neural network that transforms a set of hierarchical feature maps to another set of hierarchical features with identical dimensions. The benefit though is that the new feature maps have richer representations of the information in the image (from which the feature maps were generated). Using the processed feature maps therefore improves the performance of the models used for any of the downstream vision tasks.

When a CNN produces feature maps of various dimensions (a feature pyramid), the highest quality *scene-level* image representations can be found in the lowest resolution maps. They are therefore said to have *semantically strong representations* and can be used to extract the "meaning" of the scene. On the other hand, high-resolution feature maps, that are generated in the earlier convolution layers, are generally better at extracting local features such as edges but contain weaker scene-level information. The aim of the FPN is to transform the feature pyramid so that all the layers in the new pyramid contain strong semantic representations of the scene.

Figure 5.2 illustrates the architecture of the FPN. It consists of a bottom-up processing path, a top-down path and lateral connections between the original and intermediate feature pyramids. Although the FPN operates on an existing feature pyramid that has been generated by a backbone network, it is agnostic to the architecture of the backbone network.

The bottom-up path is the feedforward computation of the backbone network, typically one that produces a hierarchy of feature maps. In figure 5.2, the input feature maps that have been generated by the backbone are denoted as $\{C_1, C_2, C_3, C_4\}$ and have successively lower resolutions when compared to the original image. The feature maps with stronger semantic content have been indicated in figure 5.2 as ones with thicker edges. Notice that figure 5.2 indicates that all the levels of the processed pyramid are expected to have strong scene-level information.

The top-down pathway starts with the lowest resolution intermediate feature map and generates higher resolution intermediate maps by successive up-sampling. The lowest resolution intermediate map ($M_4$) is generated by applying a simple 1×1 convolution operation on the lowest resolution map of the input pyramid. While a 1×1 convolution operation does not change the

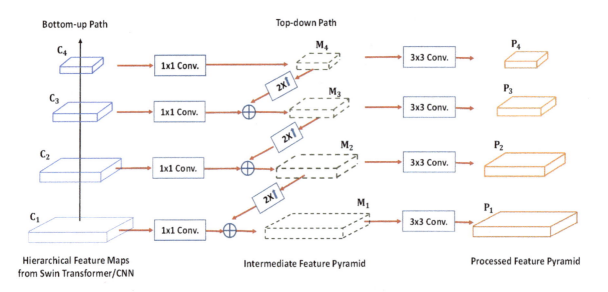

**Figure 5.2** Architecture of the Feature Pyramid Network.

spatial resolution of the feature map, it is used to modify the number of channels based on the specific implementation of this architecture. For example, in the original FPN paper [20], all the intermediate and final pyramid levels contain 256 channels of data. This number also determines the number of filters used in all of the 1×1 and 3×3 convolutional layers shown in figure 5.2. The next layer of the intermediate pyramid ($\mathbf{M_3}$) is generated by first upsampling the $\mathbf{M_4}$ feature map by a factor of two in each dimension using a simple upscaling technique like nearest-neighbor interpolation (to reduce computational complexity). Since the crude up-sampling operation reduces the accuracy of the feature locations as compared to the original feature map, the corresponding input layer ($\mathbf{C_3}$) is added back, to enhance the quality of this up-sampled version of $\mathbf{M_3}$ (say $\mathbf{M_3'}$), via a lateral connection. The $\mathbf{C_3}$ feature map is passed through a 1×1 convolutional layer to ensure that it has the same dimensions as $\mathbf{M_3'}$. The two processed feature maps are then combined using an element-wise addition operation to generate the intermediate feature map $\mathbf{M_3}$. This process is recursively used to generate the remaining layers of the intermediate feature pyramid. Note that the same 1×1 convolutional layer is used to process feature maps in all of the lateral connection paths.

Each layer of the intermediate pyramid is then processed by a 3×3 convolution layer to generate the corresponding layer in the final feature pyramid. This operation is aimed at reducing any potential aliasing artifacts that might have resulted from the up-sampling process. This final set of feature maps is denoted as $\{\mathbf{P_1}, \mathbf{P_2}, \mathbf{P_3}, \mathbf{P_4}\}$, and they have the same spatial resolution as their input counterparts. The processed feature pyramid can now be used as an input for any generic vision task.

The use of the FPN to pre-process the feature pyramid has been proven to provide a performance boost in a number of vision tasks such as object detection, semantic segmentation and instance segmentation.

### 5.2.2. Object Detection and Instance Segmentation

As mentioned earlier, in the original Swin paper [16], the Swin Transformer backbone was evaluated with the Mask R-CNN network for object detection and instance segmentation. Mask R-CNN [21] (mask region-based CNN) is a popular model used for object instance segmentation. The model can be trained to detect all the instances of a set of target object classes and it produces a pixel-level segmentation mask for each instance. The mask R-CNN architecture is illustrated in figure 5.3. As is the case with most segmentation frameworks, it consists of two convolution processing stages.

The first stage is a specialized trained CNN, known as a *region proposal network* (RPN) [22], which consists of a CNN followed by two parallel fully-connected layers. The CNN portion of the RPN is trained to generate a feature map with the same dimensions as the input image. The feature map is consumed by one of the fully-connected layers to generate candidate bounding boxes (pixel

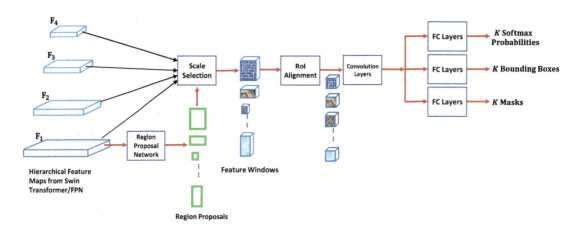

**Figure 5.3** Mask R-CNN Architecture with Hierarchical Feature Maps for Object Detection and Instance Segmentation (FC Layers = fully-connected layers, $K$ = number of object classes).

regions), each of which has dimensions that are adaptively chosen from a set of pre-determined sizes. The pre-determined windows are known as anchor boxes, and a set of 9 anchors was proposed in [22]. Each bounding box covers a region of the feature map and is known as a *region proposal*. The second fully-connected layer in the RPN generates an object score for each region proposal, which indicates the probability of having an object from one of the target classes (including a background class) in the region covered by the bounding box.

The second stage of mask R-CNN is an optimized R-CNN (region-based CNN) which uses the feature values within each region proposal to perform object classification and to generate a refined bounding box for each object in the region (via regression). The region of the feature map that is covered by each bounding box is extracted and processed to generate a fixed-length feature vector ("ROI Alignment" in figure 5.3). This ensures that the rest of the processing chain is agnostic to the size of the bounding box. Mask R-CNN then uses another convolutional network and independent fully-connected layers to produce the following outputs for each region proposal:

1. Softmax probability estimates for the target object classes and the default "background" class.
2. The location offset and dimensions of a refined bounding box for each object class.
3. A pixel-level segmentation mask for each object class over its corresponding bounding box.

Mask R-CNN is able to generate accurate masks with pixel-level granularity using a bilinear interpolation technique to uniformly sample the feature map over the extent of each window region. The probability estimation (classification) and segmentation mask generation operations are performed independently by two different fully-connected layers, thereby increasing the robustness of the results.

The Mask R-CNN model can also be used with pre-trained networks that generate one or more feature maps after processing the input image. In the case of a single feature map input, the RPN generates region proposals by directly processing the feature map, and the R-CNN stage operates as described above. When a hierarchy of feature maps is available, the modified RPN generates region proposals using the highest resolution feature map. Then, based on the size of each bounding box, the optimal scale of the input feature pyramid is chosen for the processing stages of the R-CNN portion of the network. The scale is chosen to ensure that when the bounding box at that scale is mapped back to the resolution of the original image, it has an approximately constant number of pixels. It is important to remember that the feature maps need to be computed just once for the entire image, regardless of the number of region proposals.

Figure 5.4 shows an example output from Mask R-CNN, where the network has generated a bounding box, a label and an object mask for each object of interest in the input image. It also shows the name of the class assigned to each object and the estimated class probability.

**Figure 5.4** Object Detection and Instance Segmentation using Mask R-CNN (from [21]).

The Mask R-CNN network is trained end-to-end for all the three outputs. This means that separate loss functions are used during training, in parallel, for final object classification, object bounding-box regression and object mask generation. Mask R-CNN can operate on data from either a Resnet-based CNN backbone or the Swin Transformer since both of them produce a hierarchy of feature maps. This feature pyramid could optionally be processed by an FPN before it is fed to the Mask R-CNN.

### 5.2.3. Semantic Segmentation

In [16], the Swin Transformer backbone was evaluated with the *Unified Perceptual Parsing Network (UPerNet)* for semantic segmentation. *Unified perceptual parsing (UPP)* was introduced in [23] as a step towards developing a neural network framework with the ability to simultaneously perform the most common vision tasks like classification, object segmentation, texture segmentation and semantic segmentation. It is a neural network framework that is designed to perform a variety of vision tasks using a common backbone. The challenge with such a framework is that each vision task has its own specific requirements for which the neural network will have to be trained. Moreover, the datasets that are available to train the network for each task are different in a variety of ways. The datasets contain task-specific annotations which become heterogeneous when mixed with datasets for other vision tasks. UPP addresses these problems by utilizing separate heads for each task, by selectively updating only the relevant convolution layers when training on common data and by exploiting the differing characteristics of the feature maps that make up a hierarchical representation. UPerNet is a neural network that is designed within the UPP framework.

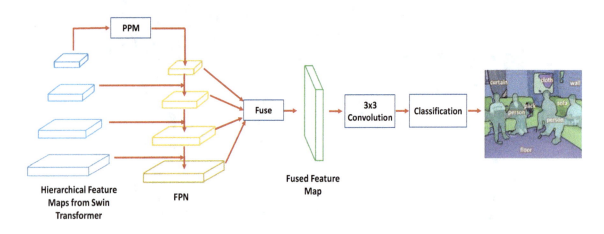

**Figure 5.5** Architecture of the Universal Perceptual Network for Semantic Segmentation (Output Image from [23]).

The UPerNet architecture for semantic segmentation is shown in figure 5.5. It follows the general UPP architecture for vision tasks and can be divided into four broad sections - a backbone network that generates a set of hierarchical feature maps, the feature pyramid network that uses a top-down architecture with lateral connections to fuse high-level semantic information into middle and low levels, a feature fusion block and a set of task-specific heads. The backbone network could be a CNN like Resnet, or a Swin Transformer, that produces a pyramid of feature maps. The feature pyramid network that was discussed in section 5.2.1 is employed in UPerNet with one modification – a *pyramid pooling module (PPM)* [24] is applied on the lowest resolution feature map in the input pyramid before it is fed into the top-down branch of the FPN. The function of the PPM is to extract the pieces of global information contained in different parts of the feature map, and to distribute this information across the features to generate an enhanced feature map. It was shown in [24] that this processing step is generally beneficial to a range of downstream tasks that use the enhanced feature map. The lowest resolution feature map in the pyramid is chosen for this kind of processing because, as discussed in section 5.2.1, this is the feature map in the pyramid that contains the highest amount of semantic information. The idea behind pyramid pooling is that different regions of the feature map capture information from non-overlapping regions in the input image, and combining these pieces of contextual information could generate a good amount of global context about the original input image. Global cues can be extracted by generating several intermediate scales of the feature map. These intermediate scales can then be fused together to generate an enhanced feature map[2].

Figure 5.6 shows the general architecture of the PPM module. The first processing step computes the average feature value over regions of varying sizes for each channel of the input feature map in order to generate several intermediate representations. Figure 5.6 shows intermediate global representations of sizes 1×1, 2×2, 3×3 and 6×6 (values used in [24]) that are generated by

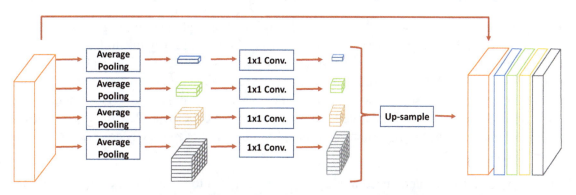

**Figure 5.6** Architecture of the Pyramid Pooling Module.

---

[2] While the PPM functions much like the FPN, the key difference is that the former processes a single feature map whereas the latter operates on a feature pyramid.

applying the appropriate average pooling schemes to the input feature map. Since these representations still have the same number of channels as the input, a 1×1 convolution is further applied to reduce the number of channels. The final representations are then spatially up-sampled such that each of them has the same spatial size as the input feature map. The output feature map is generated by concatenating in the channel dimension the original feature map with the up-sampled global representations.

In the UPerNet architecture, the PPM module is applied to the smallest feature map in the input pyramid, which could be generated by a Swin Transformer or a CNN backbone. The enhanced output is then used as the starting feature map in the top-down processing path of the FPN (see figure 5.2). The implementation in [23] used 512 channels for the output feature maps of the PPM and FPN blocks.

In the UperNet architecture of figure 5.5, the pyramid generated by the FPN is then fused into a single feature map. The fusion process begins by up-sampling the smaller feature maps to the size of the largest feature map in the pyramid and concatenating the results in the channel dimension. A trained convolutional layer is then applied to fuse features from different levels as well as to reduce the number of channel dimensions to 512. The fused feature map is processed first by a convolution layer, and then a classifier to generate the final segmentation result. Figure 5.5 also shows an example output of a semantic segmentation map from [23].

In [16], the Swin Transformer was used as the backbone network in the UPerNet architecture to generate the input set of hierarchical feature maps. It was seen that this improves the performance of semantic segmentation when compared to using traditional CNN backbones such as ResNet.

## 5.3. Image Restoration

Image restoration is a vision task whose aim is to generate a high-quality image from one or a series of low-quality image(s). The low-quality image(s) could be noisy due to low-light and/or other capture conditions or could have artifacts from down-sampling (ringing) and compression (blocking and ringing). While the central aim of image restoration is to remove these artifacts, the processed image could also be of a higher resolution when compared to the original image (as in the case of image super-resolution). While this problem has been tackled for decades using traditional image processing algorithms, recent approaches have been heavily centered around the use of CNNs.

The SwinIR model was introduced in [25] as a new approach to several image restoration tasks using the original Swin Transformer architecture. It was shown that this Swin Transformer baseline architecture serves as an excellent alternative to traditional CNN networks for three representative restoration tasks - image super-resolution, image denoising and JPEG compression artifact reduction. Section 5.3.1 discusses the structure of the generic network based on the Swin

Prajit Kulkarni

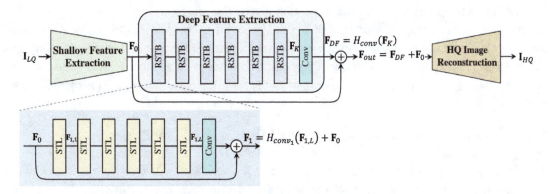

**Figure 5.7** Architecture for Image Restoration using Swin Transformers (adapted from [25]). The feature extraction modules together form the backbone network (RSTB = Residual Swin Transformer Block, STL = Swin Transformer Layer).

Transformer, and section 5.3.2 discusses the intricacies of adapting this model to specific restoration tasks.

## 5.3.1. SwinIR Architecture

As shown in Fig. 5.7, the SwinIR architecture is made up of three processing modules - shallow feature extraction, deep feature extraction and high-quality image reconstruction. The output of the shallow feature detection module is used as the basis for deep feature extraction. The outputs of the two feature extraction modules are fused via a residual connection to generate the final feature map. This feature map is processed by a CNN-based high-quality image reconstruction module.

The shallow feature module is used to extract and enhance local features, and the deep feature module is used to enhance global features in the input low-quality image. The former uses a CNN because it is able to extract mainly localized features, while the latter makes use of Swin Transformer modules due to the ability of Transformers to extract global correlations. The feature extraction modules are described in the following sections, where the input low-quality image is denoted by $I_{LQ}$, with $I_{LQ} \in \mathbb{R}^{H \times W \times C_{in}}$.

### 5.3.1.1. Local Feature Extraction

The use of a convolutional layer early in the processing chain has been seen to generally help Transformers to better capture global correlations in the images. The SwinIR model leverages this fact and applies a simple convolutional layer to the input image to generate an intermediate feature map that is further processed by a series of Swin Transformers. The input image $I_{LQ}$ is passed

96

through a single 3×3 convolutional layer to extract local features in the image. This set of $C$ 3×3 learned filters is applied to every pixel location across the image and this operation results in an intermediate feature map of size $H \times W$ pixels, but with $C$ components. Another advantage of applying this layer is that the input image can be transformed to a higher-dimensional feature space ($C \gg 3$), which provides the subsequent processing module with a richer feature set on which to operate. Denoting the resulting feature map by $\mathbf{F}_0$, we have $\mathbf{F}_0 = conv_{3\times3}(\mathbf{I}_{LQ})$, where $\mathbf{F}_0 \in \mathbb{R}^{H \times W \times C}$.

### 5.3.1.2. Deep Feature Extraction – Residual Swin Transformer Blocks

The deep feature module consists of a sequence of $K$ *Residual Swin Transformer Block* (*RSTB*) sub-modules. Figure 5.7 also shows the structure of one such sub-module. Each sub-module consists of an even number (denoted by $L$) of Swin Transformer blocks followed by a 3×3 convolutional layer. As the name suggests, it also consists of a residual connection between the input to the module and the output of the convolutional layer. All the Swin Transformer blocks generate feature maps at the fixed input resolution of $H \times W \times C$, and the ability of the Swin architecture to generate hierarchical feature maps is *not* utilized in this architecture. However, the structure of each pair of successive (chained) Swin Transformer blocks is identical to that in the Swin architecture (section 4.1.2).

The use of a convolutional layer at the end of the RSTB sub-module is thought to enhance the performance of the baseline restoration network by introducing a level of translational invariance. The residual connection provides an identity-based connection from different blocks to the reconstruction module, allowing added flexibility in aggregating features.

Denoting the feature map generated by the $k^{th}$ RSTB as $\mathbf{F}_k \in \mathbb{R}^{H \times W \times C}$, the overall processing performed by the $k^{th}$ RSTB as $H_{RSTB_k}$, the processing performed by the convolution layer after the last RSTB as $H_{conv}$ and the output of the final processing stage in the deep feature extraction block as $\mathbf{F}_{DF} \in \mathbb{R}^{H \times W \times C}$, the input feature map $\mathbf{F}_0$ goes through the following sequence of operations.

$$\mathbf{F}_1 = H_{RSTB_1}(\mathbf{F}_0)$$

$$\mathbf{F}_k = H_{RSTB_k}(\mathbf{F}_{k-1}), k = 2, \dots, K$$

$$\mathbf{F}_{DF} = H_{conv}(\mathbf{F}_K)$$

The processing performed by the $k^{th}$ RSTB, $H_{RSTB_k}$, can be further broken down into the following sequence of operations, where $H_{STL_{k,l}}$ denotes the processing performed by the $l^{th}$ Swin Transformer layer in the $k^{th}$ RSTB, $\mathbf{F}_{k,l}$ is the feature map generated by the $l^{th}$ Swin Transformer layer, $\mathbf{F}_{k-1}$ and $\mathbf{F}_k$ are respectively the feature map input to, and output from, the $k^{th}$ RSTB, and $H_{conv_k}$ is the processing performed by the convolutional layer in the $k^{th}$ RSTB.

$$\mathbf{F}_{k,1} = H_{STL_{k,1}}(\mathbf{F}_{k-1})$$

$$\mathbf{F}_{k,l} = H_{STL_{k,l}}(\mathbf{F}_{k,l-1}), l = 2, \dots, L$$

$$\mathbf{F}_k = H_{conv_k}(\mathbf{F}_{k,L}) + \mathbf{F}_{k-1}$$

As shown in figure 5.7, the Swin Transformer backbone generates a final feature map $\mathbf{F}_{out}$ by fusing the shallow and deep feature maps. The final feature map is then processed by a task-specific image reconstruction network that could take on several forms, as discussed in the next section.

## 5.3.2. Restoration Tasks

The feature map generated by the SwinIR backbone is fed to a CNN that is designed independently for each specific image restoration task. The following sections discuss the specific networks that were used in [25] for three common restoration tasks – image super-resolution, image denoising and JPEG compression artifact removal. Each network was trained using the corresponding task-specific datasets. The performance of each network was measured against the respective state-of-the-art CNNs and Transformer-based models.

### 5.3.2.1. Image Super-resolution

The task of image super-resolution combines image scaling and image enhancement. The traditional image processing approach to this task involved capturing multiple images, which differ slightly either spatially or temporally, of the same scene. The images were then fused adaptively to generate one upscaled super-resolved image with better details and fewer artifacts than any of the input images. Recent machine learning approaches use neural networks that are trained to operate on a single image input and generate an upscaled super-resolved version of that image.

The high-quality image reconstruction module for super-resolution consists of a sub-pixel convolution layer to generate an up-sampled and super-resolved version of the input image $\mathbf{I}_{LQ}$. Figure 5.8 shows the architecture of the *Efficient Sub-pixel Convolutional Neural Network (ESPCN)* that was introduced in [26]. This is a single-image super-resolution network where the input image is upscaled by a factor $r > 1$. The network consists of a series of convolutional layers followed by a sub-pixel convolution layer, which generates a feature map of size $H_{in} \times W_{in} \times r^2 C_{in}$. This feature map is then rearranged in a periodic shuffling operation to generate an output image with the expected dimensions of $rH_{in} \times rW_{in} \times C_{in}$. The shuffling operation is illustrated in figure 5.8 using colored pixels. The key advantage of this network is that it minimizes memory and computational requirements by operating the majority of the convolutional layers in the low-resolution regime of the input image, and then generates an upscaled image in the last layer. This allows the network to use spatially smaller filters in a majority of the layers, as opposed to a network that upscales the image in one of the early convolutional layers.

Starting with an input image $\mathbf{I}_{LQ} \in \mathbb{R}^{H \times W \times C_{in}}$, the SwinIR backbone generates a feature map $\mathbf{F}_{out} \in \mathbb{R}^{H \times W \times C}$, where $C$ is the number of components in the latent representation of the input image (see section 5.3.1.1). This feature map is then transformed using a CNN to reconstruct the high-resolution output image $\mathbf{I}_{HQ} \in \mathbb{R}^{rH \times rW \times C_{in}}$. The high-quality reconstruction network in this case consists of two convolution layers, with 64 5×5 filters in the first layer and 32 3×3 filters in the second layer with the hyperbolic tangent activation function applied to the output feature maps of both of these layers. They are followed by a sub-pixel convolution layer that uses $r^2 C_{in}$ 3x3 filters with no activation function. The feature map at the output of this layer, which has dimensions of $H \times W \times r^2 C_{in}$, is periodically reshuffled to generate the super-resolved output image $\mathbf{I}_{HQ}$.

It was seen that super-resolution performance initially improved with an increase in both the number of RSTB sub-modules and the number of Swin Transformer blocks in each RSTB sub-module, but quickly saturated around $K = 6$ and $L = 6$. Therefore, the final model in [25] uses 6 sub-modules and 6 Swin Transformer blocks in each RSTB sub-module. The effect of the number of channels in the intermediate representation ($C$) was also studied, and the performance improved with an increase in its number. However, since the number of parameters grows quadratically with the number of channels, a number of $C = 180$ was seen to yield the best trade-off. This architecture was used as the generic baseline for all the three image restoration tasks.

The attention window size was set to 8×8 embeddings and six attention heads ($A = 6$) were used in within for the MHSA layer. A lightweight model was also proposed for this task, where the

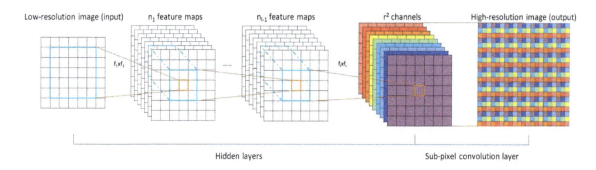

**Figure 5.8** Sub-pixel Convolutional Neural Network for Image Up-sampling (from [26]).

number of RSTB sub-modules was reduced to four ($K = 4$) and the number of channels in the latent representation was reduced to 60 ($C = 60$).

The SwinIR model was shown to produce results (measured in terms of PSNR and SSIM with respect to the ground-truth high-resolution image) that were better than those generated by networks that use pure CNNs or CNNs with attention layers and also other Transformer-based models for the 2×, 3× and 4× super-resolution cases. This was true even when the light-weight SwinIR network was used for deep feature extraction.

For the restoration tasks that do not require image upscaling, such as denoising and artifact removal, the SwinIR backbone was used to generate a *residual image*. In other words, the feature detection blocks were trained to generate a feature map that was used to reconstruct a residual image $\mathbf{I}_\Delta \in \mathbb{R}^{H \times W \times C_{in}}$. The high-quality image output was generated by adding the residual image to the original low-quality input (i.e., $\mathbf{I}_{HQ} = \mathbf{I}_{LQ} + \mathbf{I}_\Delta$).

### 5.3.2.2. Image Denoising

The baseline configuration of the SwinIR backbone was used for image denoising ($K = 6, L = 6, C = 180, A = 6$, attention window size = 8×8). However, the image reconstruction network, which generates the *residual* gray-scale and color images, is much simpler in the case of image denoising. For both the gray-scale and RGB cases, the input image is mapped to the $H \times W \times C$ intermediate representation by the SwinIR backbone. The resulting feature map $\mathbf{F}_{out} \in \mathbb{R}^{H \times W \times C}$ is processed by a single convolution layer, with 3×3 filters, to generate the residual image $\mathbf{I}_\Delta$. This layer transforms the $H \times W \times C$ feature map to a $H \times W \times 1$ gray-scale residual image or a $H \times W \times 3$ RGB residual image as required. The output denoised image is generated by adding the residual image back to the input noisy image.

This model was tested with varying amounts of additive Gaussian noise and was able to beat the performance of the state-of-the-art CNN networks for noise reduction.

### 5.3.2.3. JPEG Compression Artifact Removal

The SwinIR model was also used to remove block artifacts that result from compressing color images using a block-based algorithm such as JPEG. The baseline model configuration that was used for the image super-resolution task was also used for this task with one exception. An attention window size of 7×7 was used since an 8×8 window showed significant performance degradation (due to the use of 8×8 image block partition used during JPEG compression). A single convolution layer (with 3×3 filters) was used for reconstruction, wherein the $H \times W \times C$ feature map is processed to generate an output $H \times W \times 3$ residual color image. The high-quality output image was generated by adding this residual image to the input image.

The SwinIR model was evaluated over a range of JPEG quality factors and was seen to perform better than the standard reference CNNs designed for this task.

These results show that SwinIR architecture effectively leverages the ability of the Swin Transformer model to capture long-range correlations and the ability of a CNN to capture local correlations in order to generate a rich feature representation of the input low-quality/low-resolution image. This high-quality feature map makes it possible to reconstruct a high-quality output image or residual image using a low-complexity task-specific CNN for multiple image restoration tasks.

# References

[1] Vaswani A. *et al*., "Attention Is All You Need," Proceedings of the 31st International Conference on Neural Information Processing Systems (NIPS), December 2017, pp. 6000–6010.

[2] Choudhury A., "A Simple Approximation to the Area under Standard Normal Curve," Mathematics and Statistics, 2014, Vol. 2, pp. 147-149.

[3] Devlin J., Chang M.-W., Lee K., and Toutanova K., "BERT: Pretraining of Deep Bidirectional Transformers for Language Understanding," Proceedings of the 2019 Conference of the North American Chapter of the Association for Computational Linguistics: Human Language Technologies (NAACL-HLT), Volume 1, pp. 4171-4186, 2019.

[4] Radford A., Narasimhan K., Salimans T. and Sutskever I., "Improving Language Understanding by Generative Pre-Training," 2018.

[5] Sennrich R., Haddow B. and Birch A., "Neural Machine Translation of Rare Words with Subword Units," In Proceedings of the 54th Annual Meeting of the Association for Computational Linguistics (Volume 1: Long Papers), pp. 1715–1725, 2016.

[6] Radford A., Wu J., Child R., Luan D., Amodei D., and Sutskever I., "Language Models are Unsupervised Multitask Learners," OpenAI blog 1, no. 8 (2019): 9.

[7] Brown T. *et al*., "Language Models are Few-Shot Learners," Proceedings of Advances in Neural Information Processing Systems, Vol. 33, pp. 1877-1901, 2020.

[8] Child R., Gray S., Radford A. and Sutskever I., "Generating long sequences with sparse transformers," arXiv:1904.10509, 2019.

[9] Ouyang L. *et al*., "Training Language Models to Follow Instructions with Human Feedback," in Proceedings of Advances in Neural Information Processing Systems (NeurIPS), 2022.

[10] Dosovitskiy A. *et al*., "An Image is Worth 16x16 Words: Transformers for Image Recognition at Scale," International Conference on Learning Representations (ICLR), 2021. Online resource: arXiv:2010.11929v2.

[11] Xiong R. *et al*., "On Layer Normalization in the Transformer Architecture," Proceedings of the 37th International Conference on Machine Learning, July 2020, PMLR Vol. 119, pp. 10524-10533.

[12] Zhai X. *et al*., "A Large-scale Study of Representation Learning with the Visual Task Adaptation Benchmark," Online resource: arXiv:1910.04867.

[13] Kolesnikov A. *et al*., "Big Transfer (BiT): General Visual Representation Learning," Proceedings of the 16th European Conference on Computer Vision (ECCV), 2020, Part V, pp. 491-507.

[14] Tschannen M. *et al*., "Self-Supervised Learning of Video-Induced Visual Invariances," Proceedings of the IEEE Conference on Computer Vision and Pattern Recognition (CVPR), 2020, pp. 13806-13815.

[15] Zhai X. *et al*., "S4L: Self-supervised Semi-supervised Learning," Proceedings of the IEEE International Conference on Computer Vision (ICCV), 2019, pp. 1476-1485.

[16] Liu Z. *et al.*, "Swin Transformer: Hierarchical Vision Transformer using Shifted Windows," Proceedings of the IEEE International Conference on Computer Vision (ICCV), 2021, pp. 9992-10002.

[17] Shaw P., Uszkoreit J. and Vaswani A., "Self-attention with Relative Position Representations," Online resource: arXiv preprint arXiv:1803.02155, 2018.

[18] Liu Z. *et al.*, "Swin Transformer V2: Scaling Up Capacity and Resolution," Proceedings of the IEEE Conference on Computer Vision and Pattern Recognition (CVPR), 2022, pp. 11999-12009.

[19] Xie Z.*et al.*, "SimMIM: A Simple Framework for Masked Image Modeling," Proceedings of the IEEE Conference on Computer Vision and Pattern Recognition (CVPR), 2022, pp. 9643-9653.

[20] Lin T. -Y., Dollár P., Girshick R., He K., Hariharan B. and Belongie S., "Feature Pyramid Networks for Object Detection," Proceedings of the IEEE Conference on Computer Vision and Pattern Recognition (CVPR), 2017, pp. 936-944.

[21] He K., Gkioxari G., Doll P. and Girshick R., "Mask R-CNN," Proceedings of the IEEE International Conference on Computer Vision (ICCV), 2017, pp. 2980-2988.

[22] Ren S., He K., Girshick R., and Sun J., "Faster R-CNN: Towards Real-time Object Detection with Region Proposal Networks," In Advances in Neural Information Processing Systems, Vol. 28, 2015.

[23] Xiao T., Liu Y., Zhou B., Jiang Y. and Sun J., "Unified Perceptual Parsing for Scene Understanding," Proceedings of the European conference on computer vision (ECCV), 2018, pp. 418-434.

[24] Zhao H. *et al.*, "Pyramid Scene Parsing Network," Proceedings of the IEEE Conference on Computer Vision and Pattern Recognition (CVPR), 2017, pp. 6230-6239.

[25] Liang J. *et al.*, "SwinIR: Image Restoration Using Swin Transformer," Proceedings of the IEEE International Conference on Computer Vision (ICCV) Workshops, 2021, pp. 1833-1844.

[26] Shi W. *et al.*, "Real-time single image and video Superresolution using an Efficient Sub-pixel Convolutional Neural Network," Proceedings of the IEEE Conference on Computer Vision and Pattern Recognition (CVPR), 2016, pp. 1874–1883.

www.ingramcontent.com/pod-product-compliance
Lightning Source LLC
LaVergne TN
LVHW081531050326
832903LV00025B/1732